PRAYER GUIDE

A Manual *for* Leading Prayer

By

Lowell Snow

ISBN-13: 978-0-9776174-0-1
ISBN-10: 0-9776174-0-8

Dewey Decimal Classification: 264.7
Subject Heading: PUBLIC WORSHIP-Prayer meetings

Scripture quotations identified as NIV are from the Holy Bible, New International Version, copyright © 1973, 1978, 1984 by International Bible Society.

Scripture quotations identified as NKJV are from the Holy Bible, New King James Version, copyright © 1979, 1980, 1982 by Thomas Nelson, Inc., Publishers.

Scripture quotations identified as KJV are from the Holy Bible, King James Version.

Scripture quotations identified as TLB are from the Living Bible paraphrase of the Holy Bible, copyright © 1971 by Tyndale House Publishers, Inc.

First Edition – 2006
Second Printing - 2007
Published by
Stonehouse Creations
P.O.Box 500, Prairie Grove, AR 72753-0500

See www.lowellsnow.com to order additional copies or study materials.

Dedication

In memory of my father and mother,
Ed and Maxine Snow

My Dad was the most genuine and manly Christian I've ever known. Whether teaching a Bible class, supervising a hundred men on a construction site, or leading family devotions; he was the same Godly man. His encouragement and support were always a constant for me, no matter what direction God led. Much of this manuscript was written in his nursing home room during the last months of his life.

My mother was the example of a life lived in dedicated service to Christ. She taught Sunday School for over sixty years and worked with the girls' missionary organization until dementia robbed her of this joy at the age of 81. Her commitment to Christ and missions was so close to her heart that when she had to move to a nursing home, she thought it was the women's missionary convention and spent her last days happily going about the Father's business.

Acknowledgements

Len Goss saw the seedling of this book in an article I'd written about prayer in worship and encouraged me to broaden my perspective and write a practical 'how to' that would be helpful to all Christians.

The writing and production of Prayer Guide has been a collaborative effort with Peggy, my partner in life and ministry. She's my editor, cheerleader, researcher, proof reader, and friend.

Mike Lawrence and Maryanne Pickard were a huge help with grammatical proof reads of the final drafts.

Contents

Book Overview

The purpose of this book is to help you help others talk with God. It's a pilgrimage from the basics of saying a brief public prayer, to leading small group prayer, and concludes with guiding congregational prayer. Whether you're a new Christian, just beginning your prayer walk with God, or a veteran prayer warrior; you'll find new insights all along the way.

It's titled *Prayer Guide* because it will train you to 'guide' others into the presence of God. It's called a manual because it's intended to be used and reused through the years as you grow in your service to Christ.

Your pilgrimage of prayer will grow through three distinct stages of public prayer: saying, leading, and guiding.

> ➤ Saying your first public prayer can be one of the most frightening experiences of the Christian's life. Insights and practical guidance found in the early chapters will calm your fears. More importantly, you'll learn to become a channel of God's grace and power into any situation.
> ➤ Leading group prayer may be something you don't think you'll ever do, but virtually every follower of Christ eventually leads some form of group prayer even if it's just within their own family.
> ➤ Becoming a prayer guide is the final step of the pilgrimage. If you're ambitious for authentic, life-changing group prayer; the last three sections of this book will be a turning point for you and any group you lead in prayer.

Many different situations of prayer leadership are discussed, but all are tied together by a fundamental 'progression of prayer': Preparation, Salutation, Petition, and Benediction. Chapters related to specific types of prayer begin with a general overview of the issues then present an outline based on this 'progression of prayer'.

The Table of Contents is detailed and there's an Index to help you locate particular issues when new prayer leadership opportunities arise or a refresher is needed.

There's a study guide after every chapter and the book is arranged into five parts to facilitate study as a five week course. The five sections are easily identifiable by those seeking help with particular types of prayer leadership.

For instance, if you're new to prayer leadership and have been asked to lead prayer at some function; the first two sections will help you prepare. If you're a minister seeking to bring prayer to the heart of worship; sections three and five will be most helpful to you.

If you're pressed for time, you can go to the chapters that will be most helpful after reading the following section overviews. However, you'll be best served to read the entire book then come back and study the sections that apply directly to you.

Part One – Prayer Basics

These chapters introduce enlightening principles that underlie public and group prayer. Here, you'll begin learning the nuts and bolts of public prayer.

Part Two – Saying & Leading Public Prayer

This section is written for those who want to pray in public confidently and authentically. From saying a prayer at a sporting event to leading a simple group prayer time, each chapter can stand alone as a reference for a particular kind of public prayer.

Part Three – Group Prayer Techniques

If a prayer *leader* is to graduate to being a prayer *guide*, he or she must learn to guide others into the Lord's presence. With the techniques taught in these chapters; any prayer event can become an encounter with God.

Part Four – Guiding Group Prayer

From leading a prayer walk to guiding a large congregation in prayer for an hour or more, these chapters help you apply the techniques learned in Part 3.

Part Five – Guiding Prayer in Worship

The greatest need in many churches today is meaningful congregational prayer at the heart of worship. Applying the prayer guide concepts and techniques to this vital area of church life will return congregational prayer to its rightful place at the heart of worship.

Part One

Prayer Basics

LORD, I call to you; come quickly to me. Hear my voice when I call to you. May my prayer be set before you like incense; may the lifting up of my hands be like the evening sacrifice.

Psalms 141:1-2 (NIV)

PRAYER GUIDE by Lowell Snow

Chapter 1

Talking With God

God's Ultimate Goal

Let's be sure we have first things first. Prayer comes before salvation, both spiritually and historically.

The parent of one of the new children on the team pulls their lawn chair up next to yours and says, "I really appreciate the way you prayed before the game."

"Oh, sure, no problem."

"No, I mean it. I could tell that you care about my child and it sounded like you were actually talking to God. I mean, it wasn't like a prayer; it was more like you were talking to Him. Anyway, I appreciate it and I was wondering how you learned to pray like that."

In the conversation that follows, you learn that this person is not only new to the community, but new in their relationship to God. The next Sunday, you meet them in the church parking lot and they accompany you to Bible study and worship.

What's their prayer experience going to be? Will they hear others 'talk' to God like you did at the game or will they hear public prayers that are little more than spiritual speeches aimed in God's direction? Are they likely to be led in such a way that they'll actually learn to talk to God for themselves?

Prayer is the heart of every Christian's relationship with God. Ask a hundred followers of Christ to relate how they came to have a personal relationship with Him and the testimony of every one will involve prayer. Ask an old saint to tell you how they maintained their faith

through years of trial and tribulation and at the heart of their enduring strength you'll find a personal relationship with God nurtured in prayer.

There's nothing more important to the growth and maturity of a Christian than learning to talk with God. To what greater goal can you aspire than helping others better communicate with their Heavenly Father?

Many lament the low priority given to prayer today, but few are prepared to do anything about it. The fact that you're holding this book indicates that you're destined to be one of those few. Whether you're a soccer mom, Bible study leader, or pastor, you can learn the skills to lead prayer effectively.

Before we go further, let's be sure we have first things first. You think I'm going to say salvation, but that's not it. Yes, if you are to lead others in prayer, you certainly must be a follower of Christ, but the truth of the matter is, prayer comes before salvation, both spiritually and historically.

Spiritually, all of us must come to God as sinners in a humble prayer of faith and repentance 'before' we receive the gift of salvation. True, many people come to Christ without saying a classic 'sinner's prayer', but they aren't saved without 'communicating' in faith with the Lord.

Historically, Adam and Eve were talking to God regularly before there was ever a need for salvation. Can you imagine them walking casually with the Lord through the Garden of Eden, discussing the beauty of a flower or the uniqueness of some animal? Ultimately, that's what prayer is, a conversation with God.

Ever since sin ended His daily walks with Adam and Eve, the Heavenly Father has been doing everything necessary to bring man back into that conversational relationship.

Jesus' death on the cross was the climax of this redemption plan and made it possible for us to have a 'right' relationship with God. However, salvation isn't His ultimate goal - a personal conversational relationship is.

Did you know that God instructed the ancient Israelites to build two altars in the Old Testament temple? Everyone's familiar with the bronze altar just outside the temple where sacrifices were made, but there was a golden altar inside. Of the two, it actually had the more prominent position, directly in front of the mercy seat where the presence of God was. This altar of incense and the sweet aroma that ascended from it every day represented the people's prayers. It was the altar of prayer.

Do you remember what the Heavenly Father did immediately after Jesus died, even while his body was still on the cross? God ripped open the veil in the temple. The veil separated God's presence from what? The altar of prayer. Now, like Adam and Eve in the garden, every follower of Christ has access to the holy of holies and conversations with the Almighty. That's pretty amazing and that's His ultimate goal.

No matter how far you go as a prayer leader, never forget that the ultimate prayer is a personal conversation with the Heavenly Father. Never be satisfied to just make spiritual speeches aimed in God's direction.

The problem today is not that followers of Christ don't want to pray, they do. What they don't want is to be bored by stuffy public prayers or manipulated into praying out loud when they don't know how.

Like that parent at the ball game, people are looking for authenticity - searching for the real thing. We have it, so let's share it by becoming effective prayer guides.

STUDY GUIDE:

1. Ultimately, prayer is a _____ with God.

2. Of the two altars associated with the Old Testament temple, the altar of _____ had the more prominent position because it was located just in front of the _____ _____.

3. Jesus death on the cross made it possible for you to have a _____ relationship with God, but His ultimate goal is to have a _____ relationship with you.

Discussion question: What do you think is the difference in an authentic public prayer and what the author calls 'spiritual speeches aimed in God's direction'?

Chapter 2

Desperate for an Encounter with God

Our Ultimate Need

Instead of life-changing encounters with the Almighty, prayer has been reduced to stuffy spiritual speeches and endless discussions of prayer requests.

It began softly, growing steadily, the distant sound of men singing, echoing through the narrow cobblestone streets. As the sound grew nearer, the tamp, tamp, tamp of their marching feet could be heard.

It was sundown on Friday at this most holy Jewish shrine. As the last rays of sunlight departed Judean hills, the haunting sound of ram's horns echoed through the ancient City of Peace. This crescendo of praise reached its climax as groups of Jewish students began arriving in this world famous courtyard. Ignoring the rows of curious tourists, they marched forward, singing in the language of their ancestors.

As the throng swelled, they reached out toward a wall where millions have sought the blessings of Jehovah. Their songs of praise became fervent prayers for the 'peace of Jerusalem'. As they reached out toward this ancient foundation, some touched it, some bowed, and some even kissed the ancient stones.

The Wailing Wall, Jerusalem's icon of prayer, last remnant of a temple where once their forefathers knew the presence of God. This wall of hewn limestone separates them from Mount Moriah where Solomon's temple once stood. In that temple, the visible Shekinah Glory of God had hovered continually over the mercy seat in the gilded holy of holies.

Politics prevent them from rebuilding their temple or even worshiping where it once stood. So they weep and pray in the spot that's as close to the ancient seat of mercy as they can get: the Wailing Wall. Week after week, year after year, decade after decade, they have come - desperate for God to intervene on their behalf.

What a moving, but sad picture of faith and hope; yet average Christians must look much the same to God. They attend prayer meetings and worship services, but seldom actually encounter God. It's as if there's a wall between them and a personal conversation with the Lord.

That wall is a misunderstanding of prayer that reduces it from life-changing encounters with the Almighty to stuffy spiritual speeches and endless discussions of prayer requests.

Tourists may visit the Wailing Wall to watch a Semitic ritual, but the Jews come to pray. Keep this picture in the back of your mind, because every group you ever lead will contain some, maybe more than you think, who are desperate for an encounter with God.

STUDY GUIDE:

1. The Wailing Wall is so significant to the Jews because it's as close as they can get to the spot where the ancient _____ _____ was.

2. According to the author, the 'wall' that separates many Christians from a personal encounter with God is a misunderstanding of prayer that reduces it to stuffy _____ _____ and endless discussions of _____ _____.

Discussion question: When did you feel closest to God during the past week? Can you explain why that situation brought you close to Him?

Chapter 3

Help!

Let Your Requests be Made Known…

If you don't think you need to ask God for anything, you need an attitude adjustment.

Be anxious for nothing, but in everything by prayer and supplication, with thanksgiving, let your requests be made known to God; Philippians 4:6 (NKJV)

There's no secret meaning in the word prayer, but there are several Greek and Hebrew words translated in our English Bibles as prayer. Each has a little different meaning.

Hebrew words for prayer:

➢ **Tepilla** - in general, supplication to God, also intercession, supplication for another

➢ **Palal** - to "judge," and then "to interpose as umpire, mediator" with the general sense of prayer

➢ **`Atar,** - "to burn incense," therefore to pray to God, the prayers of the righteous being likened to incense

➢ **Lahash,** - to "whisper a prayer" uttered in a low voice

Greek words for prayer:

➢ **Enteuxis,** - confiding access to God. Gives prominence to childlike confidence, by representing prayer as the heart's converse with God

➢ **Deesis,** - prayer for particular benefits

➢ **Proseuche,** - prayer in general, not restricted as respects its contents [1]

---

[1] (all definitions are from The New Unger's Bible Dictionary. Originally published by Moody Press of Chicago, Illinois. Copyright (c) 1988.)

The word 'prayer' is an interesting word study that has been done well, many times. For our purposes, we will use this simple definition:

Prayer is communication with God by people who believe in His ability to make a difference in their lives.

Prayer involves asking:

If you don't think you need to ask God for anything, you need an attitude adjustment. In Luke 18:9-14, Jesus tells of two men who went to the temple to pray: a super religious Pharisee and a tax collector. The tax collector's prayer, "God be merciful to me a sinner," was acceptable to God while the Pharisee's was not.

If you look back at the prayer of that arrogant Pharisee, you'll see that he didn't even ask for anything. He was too self-righteous to realize that he had a need. An effective prayer leader has a keen awareness of two things: the greatness of God and the needs of those praying to Him.

It was Jesus who said:

> "Ask and it will be given to you; seek and you will find; knock and the door will be opened to you.
> Matthew 7:7 (NIV)

There's a tendency to super-spiritualize prayer today by downplaying petitions for God's help and emphasizing praise and thanksgiving. It's true that Christ taught us the importance of appreciating God's blessings and expressing that in prayer. However, this was not His emphasis. The Model Prayer begins and ends with praise (no thanksgiving), but the body of the prayer is all about asking for help.

Christians tend to pray the way their leaders pray. If the prayer leaders always pray weak prayers in which they never really ask God to do anything, the people do the same. They

eventually assume God really can't do anything, so why ask.

In later chapters you'll learn to guide people to pray prayers of praise and thanksgiving, but never lose sight of the fact that every person and group you ever lead in prayer has needs. Guide them to ask their Heavenly Father for help.

Prayer requires faith:

The benefit of strength training for our physical health is well documented. By a disciplined regimen of ever increasing resistance, the human body can develop tremendous power and stamina.

Less understood is the benefit of spiritual strength training. Do you want great spiritual power and perseverance? It will require a regimen of spiritual disciplines as challenging as the physical exercise of an athlete. At the heart of that spiritual exercise program must be a regimen of heavyweight prayer.

If you want to grow stronger in your spiritual life; lift things that are heavy in your prayer life - pray bigger than your faith.

People have big problems - they need spiritual leaders that aren't afraid to help them pray big prayers.

A prayer without faith is just words. Jesus taught that the stronger a person's faith, the more effective their prayer.

> Then the disciples came to Jesus in private and asked, "Why couldn't we drive it out?"
> He replied, "Because you have so little faith. I tell you the truth, if you have faith as small as a mustard seed, you can say to this mountain, 'Move from here to there' and it will

move. Nothing will be impossible for you."
Matthew 17:19-20 (NIV)

Like the twelve apostles, your faith probably falls short of a mustard seed, but whatever you have will grow when you plant it in the rich soil of His grace. You do that by prayer, both personal and corporate.

How then shall they call on Him in whom they have not believed? And how shall they believe in Him of whom they have not heard? And how shall they hear without a preacher?
So then faith comes by hearing, and hearing by the word of God.
Romans 10:14-17 (NKJV)

Don't get sidetracked by the word 'preacher' in verse fourteen. It's not the word for pastor. It's the general word for public crier. The public crier was someone sent into the streets to yell out information before the days of mass media.

These verses are about the importance of sharing God's truth with our voices. The primary application is to evangelism, but there's a principle here that's important for prayer leaders. People of little or no faith receive it through the words of those who know the Word of God and use their voice to share it.

In the majority of situations in which you lead prayer, there will be some with small faith. It's an amazing thing to realize that through your guidance, their faith can be strengthened.

STUDY GUIDE:

1. According to the author, the primary purpose of prayer is to praise and give thanksgiving to God, while asking for His help should be discouraged. True or False

2. In the model prayer, Jesus demonstrated that thanksgiving is the primary focus of spiritual prayer. True or False

3. Jesus taught that everyone's prayer has equal power regardless of their spiritual maturity or faith. True or False.

4. It's an amazing thing to realize that through your _____, the _____ of others can be strengthened.

Discussion question: How do you think prayer helps your faith grow?

PRAYER GUIDE by Lowell Snow

Chapter 4

Three Ways to Conduct Public Prayer

Saying - Leading - Guiding

Most people will never really talk to the Lord as long as you, the prayer leader, are praying out loud.

It's said that the most common fear is that of public speaking. Is it any surprise then that one of the most common fears among Christians is leading public prayer? In fact, some Christians neglect joining a Bible Study group for fear they'll be called on to pray.

After all, what could be more terrifying than making a public speech directed to God Almighty? What if you mess up? Surely there's a dark corner of heaven reserved for people who mishandle prayer, right? Well, probably not, but when you consider the attitude of Jesus about prayer in the house of God, those of us who've been saying public prayers for decades, would do well to revisit those early days when we had some fear about talking to God in public.

If you're concerned about offending God by some prayer foul-up, keep in mind that someone who's afraid of praying in public isn't likely to pray in a way that makes God mad. Remember that Pharisee in the previous chapter who's self-righteous prayer was rejected by Jesus? God-pleasing prayer has much to do with attitude and little to do with words.

People with a gift for public speaking will find it easier to lead public prayer, but that doesn't mean they're better at leading other people to talk to God. You can become an effective prayer leader if you have a genuine personal prayer life and a willingness to be stretched by God.

If you're not a gifted public speaker, you'll probably be glad to know that praying in public is only a small part of your work as a prayer leader. Actually, most people will never really encounter the Lord as long as you, the prayer leader, are praying out loud. They'll be listening to your prayer for a short time, perhaps trying to pray along with you, but they'll soon wander off mentally. Some will even go to sleep.

So the first principle is to keep your spoken words to a minimum. That's good news for those of you who don't like public speaking anyway and perhaps a problem for those who love it.

The next thing you need to understand is that there are three ways to conduct public prayer. Are you going to: **say** a prayer in public, **lead** a group in common prayer, or **guide** a group to pray individually? All three of these types of public prayer involve leading others and sometimes you'll use all three in the course of a prayer meeting, but there's a great deal of difference between them.

When you say a prayer, others listen. They may participate silently, but won't pray out loud. This is the most common form of public prayer.

When you lead prayer, you expect the group to participate by praying silently as you and others pray out loud. The goal is to have the whole group agreeing in prayer for the needs being expressed by those leading the prayer.

When guiding prayer, you hope to assist each person in the group to have a personal encounter with God.

1. Saying a public prayer.

➤ The occasions include church meetings, worship services, before meals, sporting events, civic clubs, work related events, etc.
➤ The group won't participate other than perhaps praying silently as you pray out loud.
➤ The primary purpose is to express the needs of the group to God.
➤ The goal is to become a channel of God's grace. Go directly to the heart of the matter. Be specific. Pray with faith. Don't preach.
➤ See chapters 6 – 9.

2. Leading a group in prayer.

➤ The occasions include Bible study groups, some meetings, family devotions, retreats, etc. when time is very limited or the group is not ready for a more intimate encounter with God.
➤ The group is expected to participate even though some may not be willing to pray out loud.
➤ The purpose is to provide a method that encourages the whole group to pray silently, in agreement as individuals are praying out loud.
➤ The goal is to involve as many of the group as possible in round-robin style monologue prayer, but keep the whole group focused and praying.
➤ See chapter 10.

3. Guiding a group to pray.

➤ The occasions include the beginning of a Bible study group, a home prayer meeting, family devotions, or prayer time during a worship service.
➤ The individuals of the group are given opportunity to pray individually.
➤ The purpose is twofold:
  ➤ Guide the group to pray together for common needs and petitions.
  ➤ Give individuals opportunity to talk to God privately.
➤ The goal is to stay in the background, guiding rather than leading.
➤ See chapters 11 – 20.

STUDY GUIDE:

1. The three ways to lead prayer are _____, _____, and _____.

2. According to the author, God pleasing prayer has much to do with _____ and little to do with _____.

3. Does a gift for public speaking insure that a person will be an effective prayer leader? Yes or No

4. Name one occasion in which you might expect to *say* a prayer. _____.

5. In *leading* prayer, the purpose is to provide a _____ that encourages the whole group to pray together _____ as individual members of the group are praying _____ _____.

6. When *guiding* prayer, your goal is to stay in the _____.

Discussion question: Give an explanation of the three ways of conducting public prayer in your own words?

Chapter 5

The Progression of Prayer

Preparation – Salutation – Petition – Benediction

This progression represents the natural flow of conversation with God, not rules governing it.

One element of a good devotional life that carries over into being a good prayer guide is having an understanding of the progression of prayer. Prayer will generally have these four parts:

➢ Preparation
➢ Salutation
➢ Petition
➢ Benediction

This progression represents the natural flow of conversation with God, not rules governing it. It's as inherent in prayer as saying hello and goodbye is in friendly conversation.

It's not offensive to God if you don't follow this progression; we've already seen that the attitude of your heart is what He really cares about, but we're going to use it throughout the book as an easy to remember framework on which to build prayer.

Preparation:

When you pray, your prayers actually enter the throne room of Heaven. Almighty God is taking the time to listen to what you say. Does that make prayer important enough to be worthy of preparation?

Of course it does, but think about the last three times you led prayer. Did you make any preparation?

Now think about the public prayers you've heard recently. How much importance was given to them? Were they bookends for the beginning and end of a meeting or perhaps just the signal for everyone to sit or stand during a worship service?

Many have fallen into the trap of using prayer as no more than a line-item on the weekly bulletin or the opening and closing remarks for a meeting. They give it little or no thought and some even use it as a time killer.

I was invited to preach a missions emphasis in a good sized church. The church administrative pastor met me in the lobby when I arrived and helped me get situated. As I looked over the order of service, I asked if I'd have an opportunity to lead prayer during the service. He said, "Oh yes, we need you to pray right before you preach so the orchestra can leave the stage during the prayer."

When it came time, I just dismissed the orchestra and prayed later, but using prayer in this way was their normal procedure. Does the creator of the universe have to put up with that? Is that even prayer? Try to visualize that kind of prayer from God's point of view.

In another service, I was sitting in a pulpit chair on the platform when the pastor called on a layman in the congregation to pray. While the layman was praying, the pastor decided to get ready for the next segment of the service, which was a solo. There were two microphone stands, one right beside my chair and the other closer to the podium. As the layman prayed, the pastor picked up the mike nearest him and adjusted it to an appropriate height.

By the time the layman finished praying, the pastor was back behind the podium, eyes closed, looking very prayerful. When the layman said amen, he and everyone else in the auditorium glared at me for being such an inconsiderate heathen. You see, the pastor was elderly and hard of hearing. He didn't realize that the microphone he was adjusting and moving around was turned on the whole time. Everyone (who didn't peek) thought I was making all that noise during the prayer.

All of us who've been part of church life can relate humorous stories about public prayer. They may be fun to tell but illustrate the low value sometimes given to prayer.

Proper preparation will lift your prayers from the realm of the mundane to the throne room of God. Here are three preparations you should always make:

> **Invite the group to pray.**
> **Remember who you're talking to.**
> **Ask yourself, "Why am I here?"**

Sometimes, you know ahead of time that you're going to lead in prayer. We'll talk about preparations for that situation in later chapters.

More often, you're called on to pray with no warning at all. Here's how these three preparations can work together in that most common situation.

Start by 'inviting' the group to bow their heads. If the group is noisy, as they often are at the beginning of a meeting or service, speak loudly and ask for their attention. When you have their attention, say something like, "Please bow your heads with me for prayer. As you bow, please turn your attention toward the Lord."

This sets the stage for the prayer. Do not say something like this, "As you bow, put the cares of your life aside and don't think about what's going on around you." That gives them the "red-cow" syndrome. By telling them what not to think about, you've made them think about it.

Now that they know you're going to lead in prayer, you have a few seconds to collect your thoughts as the group quiets down and turns their thoughts toward God. You do not have to pray immediately.

As you wait, imagine yourself in the throne room of Heaven, on your knees before God, with the rest of the group on their knees behind you. With that picture in your mind, ask yourself, *why have we come here?* That's, why have we come into the throne room of God? What have we come here to talk to Him about or ask Him to do?

The answer to that question, why have we come here, becomes the focus of your prayer. For instance, if you're asked to say the closing prayer for your Sunday School class, the answer might be that the group needs to go into their work week and apply what they've just learned from scripture. That would become the central issue of your prayer.

We'll talk later about how the different types of prayer determine how you proceed, but do you see how making this simple preparation can bring prayer into its proper perspective? It can be the difference in talking to God and just saying a spiritual speech aimed in His direction.

Salutation:

When you write a letter, you start with a salutation. Jesus taught us to do the same when we pray. It's the respectful thing to do.

Have you ever heard a prayer leader begin public prayer in such a quick and casual way that you wondered if they had any concept of actually entering the presence of God? I've seen Bible study leaders and even ministers begin prayer so abruptly they didn't even have time to bow their own head until they were at least a sentence into the prayer. It's fairly certain that they were just filling a slot in a routine rather than talking with the Almighty.

When Jesus taught his followers how to pray, He instructed them to begin with a salutation that expressed reverence to their Lord and Creator. In the Sermon on the Mount, He gave this example:

"Our Father in heaven, hallowed be your name," Matthew 6:9 (NKJV)

In this first phrase of the model prayer, the Lord shows you three things about the salutation.

First, He's teaching you to identify to whom you are praying. Whether you're praying in your own Bible study class or over the loud speaker at a sporting event, there must be no doubt. As a Christian, you should never agree to pray a politically correct or religion neutral prayer. Thousands upon thousands of your brothers and sisters in Christ have been martyred because they would pray only to God. Keep that in mind and you'll not take this part of your prayer lightly.

Second, Jesus is teaching you to give honor to God before you talk to Him about your needs. Depending upon the situation, this may be a major portion of the prayer, but usually it's just a few words of praise.

Third, He's teaching you to address God as your Father. Jesus never made an issue of this, but it was His practice. The only time in scripture that He didn't direct His prayer to the Father was when He cried out from the cross, "My God, My God, why have you forsaken me?"

There are many honorable names in scripture that you can use to salute God as you begin your prayer, but as a daily habit, *Father*, was Jesus' choice.

Petition:

Let your requests be made known to God; Philippians 4:6b (NKJV)

The dictionary says that a petition is a solemn supplication or request to a superior authority. As a prayer leader, that's what you're trying to help others do.

Prayer petitions will fall into two broad categories: those for personal needs and those for the needs of others.

Petitions for personal needs

Expressing our heart's desire is what prayer is all about. Depending on the kind of prayer you're leading, this can be one sentence and last a few seconds, or it can include the prayers of many people and last an hour or more.

Some time ago my brother, who lives halfway across the country, was in town for a visit. My ninety-one year old widowed father lived close to me so we all got together for burgers and ice-cream at my house. My brother and I talked about kids, grandkids, our ministries - and by the end of the evening had solved most of the world's problems.

Dad sat quietly, just listening. He's never been much of a talker. That night, as I drove him home, he said, "That was wonderful. I just love listening to you two talk."

Of course he does: we're his children. The same is true of the Heavenly Father. He loves to hear His children talk, because what they talk about reveals their heart.

When I was a child, my family always had supper together. During the meal my mother labored to drag the events of the day out of the rest of us. I never understood that until I had children of my own and my wife began the same routine. As parents, we don't just want to know the events of our children's daily lives; what we're really trying to find out is what they're feeling, thinking, and needing.

In his last year of life, my father couldn't do much, but he regularly asked me how I was doing and if I needed anything. The Heavenly Father is omnipotent, but like my father, He constantly wants His children to talk to Him about what they are doing, feeling, thinking, and needing.

You may be thinking that this sounds like a self-centered kind of praying, but as you lead prayer, never forget that everyone has needs that they need to talk to their heavenly Father about - and He wants to hear from them.

I believe that one of the greatest deficiencies in the prayer life of most groups is that individuals are not led to express their deepest feelings and fears to the Lord.

Petitions for the needs of others

1. Praying for each other –

When you lead others in prayer, you want to help them pray for each other. Over and over the scripture admonishes us to support one another with wise counsel, compassion, and prayer. Consider this amazing passage written by James the brother of Jesus.

> Is anyone among you suffering? Let him pray. Is anyone cheerful? Let him sing psalms. 14 Is anyone among you sick? Let him call for the elders of the church, and let them pray over him, anointing him with oil in the name of the Lord. 15 And the prayer of faith will save the sick, and the Lord will raise him up. And if he has committed sins, he will be forgiven. 16 Confess your trespasses to one another, and pray for one another, that you may be healed. The effective, fervent prayer of a righteous man avails much.
> James 5:13-17 (NKJV)

That passage stretches the limits of my understanding of group prayer, how about you? If you want to dive into all that this passage involves, you'll have to look beyond this book. My purpose in putting it here is to impress upon you that God has thrown open the doors of his arsenal of power to faithful Christians who pray with, and for, each other.

2. Praying for kingdom needs -

Next, our petitions should include prayer for kingdom needs. The Lord has made it clear that eternal things are more important than temporal, yet many of his followers spend most of their prayer energy on earthly things.

In his booklet, *Biblical Patterns for Powerful Church Prayer Meetings[2]*, Dr. Gregory R. Frizzell, identifies *ten key kingdom issues* that you should regularly bring to your group's attention:

> ➤ Specific confession and repentance from personal and corporate sin
> ➤ Lost people and backslidden individuals.
> ➤ Sweeping revival and spiritual awakening
> ➤ Missionaries, mission initiatives and unreached people groups
> ➤ Specific church needs and ministry initiatives
> ➤ Key denominational needs, ministries and leaders
> ➤ Government, educational and cultural leaders
> ➤ Sick, bereaved, widowed, orphaned, financial needs, etc.

[2] Biblical Patterns for Powerful Church Prayer Meetings by Gregory R. Frizzell, Copyright 1999, published by The Master Design, Memphis, TN, pg 43

➢ Prayer for God to raise up many soul winners, pastors, teachers, missionaries, etc.
➢ Prayer for persecuted believers

It would be a rare prayer time in which all of these needs were addressed, but every time you lead a group to pray, remind them of needs that fall within at least two or three different categories. If you lead the same group regularly, over time, you'll want to lead them to pray for all of these issues.

Benediction:

Don't be afraid to pray a short prayer.

Pray an authentic prayer - then conclude it. You're not heard in the throne room of God for your "much speaking" (Matthew 6:7)

The benediction is the final part of prayer that redirects our attention to the Lord. Let's consider a few Biblical benedictions.

The oldest fragment of scripture in existence is a hand written copy of the Aaronic Benediction. You'll remember that these words were given to Moses by God with the specific instructions to use them for 'blessing' the people.

At the conclusion of a service, Aaron would raise his hands and say:

> The Lord bless you and keep you;
> The Lord make His face shine upon you, And be gracious to you;
> The Lord lift up His countenance upon you, and give you peace." '
> Numbers 6:24-26 (NKJV)

One of my favorite benedictions is:

> Let the words of my mouth and the meditation of my heart
> Be acceptable in Your sight,
> O LORD, my strength and my Redeemer. Ps 19:14 (NKJV)

Perhaps the most commonly used New Testament benediction is one used by Paul:

> The grace of the Lord Jesus Christ, and the love of God, and the communion of the Holy Spirit be with you all. Amen.
> 2 Corinthians 13:14 (NKJV)

One of the most beautiful New Testament benedictions is found at the conclusion of the little book of Jude:

> To him who is able to keep you from falling and to present you before his glorious presence without fault and with great joy - to the only God our Savior be glory, majesty, power and authority, through Jesus Christ our Lord, before all ages, now and forevermore! Amen.
> Jude 24-25 (NIV)

The amazing doxology of praise at the end of the third chapter of Ephesians is particularly appropriate for worship because of the reference to the church:

> Now unto him that is able to do exceeding abundantly above all that we ask or think, according to the power that worketh in us,
> Unto him be glory in the church by Christ Jesus throughout all ages, world without end. Amen.
> Eph 3:20-21 (KJV)

Christ's entire model prayer is often recited as a benediction:

> Our Father which art in heaven,
> Hallowed be thy name.
> Thy kingdom come. Thy will be done
> in earth, as it is in heaven.
> Give us this day our daily bread. And
> forgive us our debts, as we forgive
> our debtors.
> And lead us not into temptation, but
> deliver us from evil:
> For thine is the kingdom, and the
> power, and the glory, for ever. Amen.
> Matthew 6:9-13 (KJV)

These are just a few of the well known scriptural benedictions. The Bible is actually full of verses that can be used as benedictions and you'll begin to notice them once you get 'tuned-in' to this aspect of prayer.

A common benediction today, "In Jesus' name," is an application of the following verse:

> If you ask anything in My name, I will
> do it.
> John 14:14 (NKJV)

Like the other parts of the progression of prayer, there's no commandment in scripture to have a benediction. It's simply a natural conclusion to a conversation with God. In other words, if you realize at lunch that you forgot to say a benediction to your morning devotions, you need not worry that Jesus has been offended.

Neither does a benediction add power or authority to your prayer. In fact, that became a problem with the Aaronic Benediction listed above. After time, people began to think saying those words at the conclusion of a prayer made God more likely to give them what they wanted.

The same is true today with the John 14 benediction, "In Jesus' name." When you study this passage, you realize that Jesus was not actually giving us a benediction for prayer, but teaching us a principle about prayer. For our understanding, it could be paraphrased, "In Jesus' will."

The following verse describes the reason many prayer requests are turned down by God:

> You ask and do not receive, because
> you ask amiss, that you may spend it
> on your pleasures.
> James 4:3 (NKJV)

As we mature in faith and our desires become more and more in line with the desires of Christ, our prayers are more likely to be answered in the affirmative because they are more likely to be in line with the will of God.

A benediction to public prayer accomplishes two things. It honors God and it lets the group know that the prayer is over. Most Christians who lead public prayer have a favorite benediction. It doesn't matter which you use as long as it honors God and lets the group know that you have concluded the prayer.

STUDY GUIDE:

1. The progression of prayer includes: _____, _____, _____, and _____.

2. According to the author, every prayer must include all four parts or God is likely to be offended. True or False

3. When called on to pray, make these three preparations, _____ the group to pray, remember who you're _____ _____, and ask yourself, "Why am I _____?"

4. A good preparation for prayer is to imagine yourself in the _____ _____ of God.

5. One thing that reminds us of the importance of the salutation is that many Christians have been _____ rather than say a politically correct prayer.

6. Praying for the sick should be the primary focus of prayer in the church. True or False

7. Benedictions were common in both the Old and New Testaments. True or False

8. An accurate paraphrase of the common benediction, 'In Jesus name' would be 'In Jesus _____.'

Discussion question: Of the four parts of the progression, which do you think is most important and why?

Part Two

Saying & Leading Public Prayer

ow it came to pass, as He was praying in a certain place, when He ceased, that one of His disciples said to Him, "Lord, teach us to pray..."
Luke 11:1 (NKJV)

Chapter 6

Saying a Prayer in Public

Sporting Events, Civic Clubs, etc.

There's nothing more Christ-like than being Christ-like in the world.

From time to time, you'll be asked to pray in a non-church situation. This could be a sporting event, civic organization, or even the funeral for a non-Christian. Whatever the situation, remember that you're going into the presence of the Heavenly Father and talking to Him on behalf of folks that need His help.

Before we get into the actual prayer, let's consider your attitude about it. It can be aggravating to say a prayer in a situation where you know many don't care and aren't paying attention. Should you consider it an opportunity to bear witness for Christ or just reject the opportunity altogether? Neither. Consider these words from the prayer of Jesus for his followers just before he went to the cross:

> I have given them your word and the world has hated them, for they are not of the world any more than I am of the world. **My prayer is not that you take them out of the world** but that you protect them from the evil one. They are not of the world, even as I am not of it. Sanctify them by the truth; your word is truth. As you sent me into the world, **I have sent them into the world.**
> John 17:14-19 (NIV)

There's nothing more Christ-like than being Christ-like in the world. You're commissioned by Jesus to go into the world, not live in a monastery. Our society is disintegrating for lack of genuine Christians in the mainstream, so never turn down an opportunity to carry God's grace into situations away from the church.

The only exception would be if you're asked to pray a religion-neutral prayer in which you're instructed to pray to an unidentifiable 'higher power'. The person asking you to do this probably hasn't thought through the ramifications of a Christian praying in this way. Explain that millions of Christians have been killed for refusing to pray 'politically correct' prayers so you won't dishonor them or the Lord Jesus by praying in this fashion.

My brother was asked to pray before congress in Washington DC. A manuscript of the prayer was required and he provided it. Just minutes before entering, the manuscript was handed back to him with the instruction to leave out the last paragraph because it included the name of Jesus in the benediction. He asked whether they really wanted him to pray or not, but they insisted. He complied by removing the name of Jesus from the last paragraph and putting it in the first.

Interestingly, when he later looked up the transcript of his prayer on the congressional web site, the name of Jesus had been removed altogether. Don't they call that revisionist history?

We believe in freedom of religion, not from religion. I can accept that if my child is allowed to pray in 'Jesus' name' at the graduation this year, someone else's child may pray to Allah next year. I can live with that, but in a free society no one should be forced to pray a religion neutral prayer.

Billy Graham is a master of the public prayer, and that's why he's asked to pray in situations where no other evangelistic preacher would even be considered. When you see him pray in public, you're impressed with two things: he truly cares about the needs of the people he's praying for and there's no doubt to whom he's praying.

No person alive has presented the gospel to more people than he, but he doesn't manipulate public prayers into preaching opportunities.

What would you think of a minister who concluded his pre-football game prayer this way? "…And please help all those people who don't go to church to have their children in Sunday School at the Holy Light Church at the corner of 7th and Sanctuary Street, at 9:30 a.m. this Sunday morning so they can receive their own John 3:16 cherry sucker that says right on the side, For God so loved the world that He gave His only begotten son, that whosoever believeth in Him might have everlasting life, amen."

I made that up, but I've heard worse from servants of Christ who had a heart for reaching souls, but lacked an understanding of public prayer. They manipulated public prayer to their own purpose.

**When you pray in public,
pray for them not about
them.**

Praying in public may be a witness to others, but it was not created by God for that purpose. Prayer is communicating with the Almighty and should never be depreciated into announcements and promotions.

Let's say you're standing on the sideline before your child's soccer game. The coach comes up and asks you to pray for the players before the game. What's your attitude going to be?

In the back of your mind, your ungodly pride could be saying, "He should be asking me to coach, not just pray." But, if you're in the habit of remembering what public prayer really is, (going into the presence of God on behalf of folks who need His help) you look him in the eye and say, "Thanks coach, I really appreciate the opportunity."

Preparation:

- Ask them to bow their heads for prayer. Speak loudly enough to be heard and say your words clearly.
- Imagine yourself in the throne room of Heaven on your knees before God with this group of people behind you.
- Consider the group and ask yourself, *Why are we here?* (in the throne room) In other words, what does this group want you to talk to God about? The answer to that question will be the focus of your prayer.
    Note - You're not praying about what you perceive to be their need (that's preaching), but what they perceive to be their need.

Salutation:

- ➢ Begin the prayer with, "Dear Heavenly Father…"
- ➢ Give honor to God by giving praise or thanksgiving for something that the group can identify with like our nation, the good weather, our children, etc.

Petition:

- ➢ Get quickly to the heart of the matter. State the need clearly and specifically to the Lord. Don't be afraid to put God on the spot, He can handle it.
- ➢ Pray for what they expect you to pray for. If it's the safety of their children during a football game, pray that in faith, believing. That's why you're there. As a person of faith who's walking in the way of Christ, you have the ability to be a channel of God's power into that situation. Don't miss that opportunity by praying a generalized prayer that means nothing.
- ➢ Pray for secondary needs of the group, but without much elaboration. For instance, if the nation's at war, you'll certainly pray for the troops.
- ➢ Keep your public prayer brief and to the point. Beyond thirty seconds, their minds begin to wonder unless you're expressing a deeply felt need that's right at the surface of their consciousness. Of course, this is affected by the circumstance. You can take longer at a funeral than a football game.

Benediction:

- ➢ "In the name of Jesus Christ we pray, amen." Leave no doubt about who made this prayer possible.

Sample prayers:

Here's an example of a thirty-second football game prayer:

> "Dear Heavenly Father, We thank you for the opportunity to be here tonight and we want to thank you for these children. They are precious gifts from your hand. We pray for your blessing and guidance on their lives as they grow up in these difficult times. Father we are concerned for the safety of the young men that will be playing tonight. We ask that you watch over them and keep them from harm. In the name of Jesus Christ we pray, amen."

In public prayer, you'll not be heard for your "much speaking" (Matthew 6:7), either in the throne room of Heaven or among the people you're leading. Rather, the effectiveness of your prayer will be directly related to your confidence before God and your ability to express needs clearly.

Here's an example of a forty-five second opening prayer for a civic club meeting:

> "Dear Heavenly Father, We thank you for this day of life. We are thankful for health sufficient to be together. We thank you for our country and the liberty that we enjoy. We acknowledge that everything good in our lives originated with you and we praise you.
>
> Lord, these are difficult times for some of us. We pray for each other as we face the struggles of life. We also ask renewed health for those who are absent today because of sickness.
>
> We have come together today because we desire to be a blessing to our community. We ask your help and direction as we meet today. Help us be patient in our deliberations and wise in our decisions.
>
> In the name of Jesus Christ we pray, amen."

In the actual situation you would probably pray more specifically, but the point is to:

➢ Give honor to God in your salutation.
➢ Express the felt needs of the group to the Lord.
➢ Give honor to God in your benediction.

If you can guide a group of people in a secular situation close enough to God that they feel the breath of His Spirit, you have done much more than that preacher who manipulated John 3:16 onto a loudspeaker.

STUDY GUIDE:

1. When you say a public prayer you are talking to God on behalf of folks who _____ _____ _____.

2. When you pray in public, pray _____ them not _____ them.

3. Public prayer should never be depreciated into _____ or _____.

Discussion question: Did you agree or disagree with the statement, 'You're not praying about what you perceive to be their need (that's preaching), but what they perceive to be their need.'? Why?

Chapter 7

Saying an Opening or Closing Prayer

Meetings, Classes, etc.

"Why are we here?"

When asked to say an opening or closing prayer, you'll be saying the prayer while the members of the group follow your lead, praying the same prayer silently. That's the ideal, but you'll need to be an effective prayer leader to make it happen that way.

We all desire God's blessing and direction in the meetings we have, whether the group is studying the Bible or planning the budget. The problem is, we've done it so many times that these prayers have become mechanical. They're more like little speeches that express good intentions.

The next time you're in a meeting that opens or closes with prayer, pay attention to the words of the prayer and the actions of the group. Think of the prayer leader on their knees before God in the throne room of heaven with the rest of the group on their knees behind them. Ask yourself, does that mental picture fit what's really going on? Probably not. In fact, if you peek, you're likely to see folks adjusting clothes, fixing make-up, looking over their notes, or a hundred other things that demonstrate that they're not engaged in prayer.

The person leading the prayer may be just as preoccupied. This may be an unredeemed part of my personality, but I often observe people as they begin their public prayers. I trust God will forgive me because this *research* will be used for the greater good of the Kingdom.

I especially like to observe preachers. Remember I am one so give me a little slack. I recently saw a pastor begin a prayer at the beginning of his sermon like this; he asked the congregation to bow their heads and quickly began his prayer with a typical salutation. About three sentences into the prayer, he must have wondered how much time he had to preach his sermon because he brought his watch up in front of his face and checked the time as he continued to pray.

It's not just preachers. On numerous occasions I've observed a Bible teacher say a quick prayer while they continue to arrange or pack-up their materials.

These servants of Christ can do these things as they pray because their prayers are just spiritual speeches they've said hundreds of times. They follow the progression of a prayer, are

39

directed toward God, and are said with an element of faith, so are they prayers? Yes, just barely. But if you were satisfied with that, you probably wouldn't be reading this book. There is a better way.

We probably need to stop here for a moment and make clear that our purpose isn't to turn every committee meeting into a prayer meeting. An opening or closing prayer is just that, a prayer at the beginning or end. But it is prayer.

Saying an Opening Prayer

You've found a seat around a table with the other members of the student ministry team and you're chatting with the person next to you. The youth pastor calls the meeting to order and asks you to pray.

As a good prayer leader, you instinctively remember what public prayer is: talking to God about the needs of this group. You also know that the group is about to zone-out unless you can actually lead them into the throne room of God.

Preparation:

> Ask the group to bow their heads for prayer.
> Ask them to think about the task at hand. (In the situation above, you would ask them to think about the students.)
> Give them time to focus by waiting a few seconds before you actually begin your prayer.
> Use this little interlude of silence to imagine yourself on your knees in the throne room of God with the group on their knees behind you.
> Ask yourself, *Why are we here?* There are three aspects of this question.
> > First, *why* are we here? Prayer is communicating with God. Often, in a committee meeting you actually

have an agenda. The group needs God's help with those tasks.
> Second, the question is why are *we* here? not why am I here? You'll be praying on behalf of the group, not yourself.
> Third, it's why are we *here*, in the throne room of heaven? not why are we here in this committee meeting? You will pray specifically for the meeting, but if you forget that you're actually leading the group into His presence, your prayer may become more of a motivational speech than a conversation with God.

Salutation:

> Begin the prayer with, "Dear Heavenly Father…"
> Give honor to God with praise or thanksgiving for something that the group can identify with like God's love expressed through the beauty of the day, a recent life-changing commitment to Christ, a recent sacrificial gift or work done in support of this committee, a recent successful event, etc.

Petition:

> Get quickly to the heart of the matter. Whatever was on your heart when you asked the question, *why are we here*, becomes the focus of your petition to God. Make the petitions as specific as possible.
> Pray for secondary needs of the group, but without much elaboration.
> Focus on this meeting. Don't pray for the needs of individuals in the group unless you've been specifically asked to.

The same is true for the broader needs of the church.

➤ Keep your prayer brief and to the point. Don't be afraid to pray a short prayer. Jesus made it clear that we are not heard for our "much-speaking". (Matt. 6:7)

Benediction:

➤ "In Jesus' name we pray, amen."

Sample Prayer:

This is a sample of how a committee member might lead the opening prayer of the meeting mentioned above.

> "Dear Heavenly Father, thank you for the opportunity to minister to the students of our church through the work of this ministry team. What a joy it was to learn today that we had several visitors at the mid-week service. Thank you for our student pastor. Bless his family and his ministry. Thank you for the people who are working faithfully to lead and teach the Bible study groups.
>
> Lord, there are several things on our agenda, but none more important than planning next summer's mission trip. There are so many issues to be resolved, and we want more than anything to be in your perfect will. We know that there are several opportunities. Please show us the one that's right for our students.
>
> In Jesus' name we pray, amen."

Saying a Closing Prayer

The meeting has gone longer than anyone wanted or expected. Everyone seems anxious to leave and the leader calls on you to close the meeting with prayer. He's called on you because he's come to know that you won't just say a little spiritual speech while everyone gets their stuff together. You can be trusted to really pray for the needs at hand.

As you consider the focus of this prayer, you'll be looking backward and forward: backward at the meeting for unresolved issues that need God's direction and forward for His help in implementing what has been discussed or taught.

Preparation:

➤ Ask the group to bow their heads for prayer.
➤ Continue by asking them to focus their attention on the Lord.
➤ Give them a few seconds before you continue with the salutation. Silence is a good way to get folks to stop talking and fiddling with their stuff.
➤ Imagine yourself on your knees in the throne room of God with the group on their knees behind you.
➤ Ask yourself, *Why are we here?* Remember, the question isn't why are we here in this meeting, but why have we come to the throne room of God. What do we need His help with? For instance, your flower committee doesn't need God to decorate the sanctuary for them, but after a long tedious planning meeting, they might need His help remembering why they're doing it.

Salutation:

➤ Begin the prayer with, "Dear Heavenly Father…"
➤ Give honor to God with praise or thanksgiving for something related to the meeting you've just had.

Petition:

- ➢ Get quickly to the heart of the matter. Whatever was on your heart when you asked the question, *why are we here*, becomes the focus of your petition to God. Be as specific as possible. Pray in faith, knowing God can do anything He chooses to do.
- ➢ Pray for secondary needs of the group, but without much elaboration.
- ➢ Do not pray for individual or church needs unless you've been asked to do so or those needs have been discussed by the group during the meeting.

Benediction:

- ➢ "In Jesus' name we pray, amen."

Sample Prayer:

This is a sample of how a class member might lead the closing prayer in a Bible study group. For sake of illustration, assume that the class has just studied the passage from Genesis about Cain and Abel. Notice how the prayer leader looks backward to pray about the issue raised, then forward to pray about applying those issues in life.

"Dear Heavenly Father. We praise you for your Word. It truly shows us the way of life. Thank you for our teacher. We pray for your blessing on him and his family.

Lord, it is the desire of our hearts to be pleasing to you in all that we say and do. As always, your Word has challenged us to be more like you and reminded us of how often we fail.

Forgive us for being presumptuous toward you like Cain. We think we're so smart that we sometimes second-guess your commands, then get angry and frustrated when doing things our way doesn't work.

Lord, we want to do right, but sometimes we get so confused. Please help each of us see anything in our lives that is not being done the way you want it done, then help us have strength and courage to change it. Thank you for your mercy and your help.

In Jesus' name we pray, amen."

STUDY GUIDE:

1. You want to lead so that the group will follow, praying _____, the same prayer you're praying out loud.

2. Many opening and closing prayers are more like little _____ that express good _____.

3. Once you've asked people to bow their heads, you must begin praying immediately. True or False

4. When you ask yourself the question, 'Why are we here?' The 'here' means the throne room of heaven. True or False

Discussion question: Why do you think we have opening and closing prayers?

PRAYER GUIDE by Lowell Snow

Chapter 8

Saying a Prayer During a Worship Service

Offertory, Benediction, etc.

Generally, you can think of these prayers as blessings.

We are talking here about situation-specific prayers, not the prayer time or pastoral prayer. This could be the offertory prayer, benediction, or any prayer during the service that has a specific purpose.

Before we consider the prayer itself, let's think about being heard.

Using a Microphone

When leading prayer in an auditorium or any large room, it's best to use a microphone. I wonder what it says about our attitude toward prayer when we ask someone to lead a public prayer, but don't give them a microphone so people can hear what they say.

And don't be one of those folks that says, "Oh, I talk loud, everybody can hear me." Probably not. The issue isn't about being loud, it's about being understood. Big rooms have a way of garbling sound. Just use the mike.

If you're afraid of microphones, that's certainly understandable. They have a tendency to squeal, make your voice sound like you're in a cave, or not work at all. Besides that, they're a distraction. Your voice being amplified from the sound system a millisecond after you speak is confusing to your brain.

If you anticipate having to use a microphone from time to time, look for opportunities to play with one. Yes, I said play. That's how you learn. Just because you're not a child anymore, doesn't mean you don't still learn by playing. That's why you still can't operate your video recorder and a five-year-old can. If you believe prayer is important, you'll do what's necessary to be heard by every person in the congregation.

When you use a microphone, be sure it's pointed at your mouth, not the ceiling. Almost all hand-held microphones are made to receive sound from the top, not the sides. Hold it about an inch from your mouth with the cord end pointed away from your mouth, not toward the floor.

Holding a microphone too far from your mouth causes the sound man to have to turn it up too much. That leads to an irritating squeal, called 'feedback'. It's also important to never let the top of the mike point at a sound system speaker; that also can cause it to squeal. This feedback is caused when the mike is turned up so much that it begins to amplify not just your voice, but the sound coming out of the sound system speakers. This creates a loop of sound between the speaker and mike that gets louder and louder.

Praying without a microphone

Sometimes you'll not have the option of using a microphone, even though you're in a large room. There are a couple of things to consider in this situation: the size of the room and the type of room.

The size of the room

The first issue isn't so much the size of the room as how far you are from the person most distant from you. If you're in Madison Square Garden with five people gathered in a circle around you, unless there's a great deal of background noise, those five people will be able to understand your words fairly easily.

However, if you're in the church auditorium with those same five people scattered out across the room, it's much more difficult.

➢ Get them to move close to you and close together.
➢ Make eye contact with the person farthest away and speak to them. Keep this person in mind even when you're praying so that you'll continue to speak loudly enough for them to hear.

➢ Keep your face up. Don't pray toward the floor.
➢ Speak clearly. Speaking clearly is more important than speaking loudly.
   ➢ If people often have a hard time understanding you, you're probably not speaking clearly. Go home and practice in front of a mirror. Watch your mouth as you speak. Could a deaf person read your lips easily? If not, you're not speaking clearly.

The type of room (echo)

Next, consider if the room is *alive* or *dead*. A gymnasium is said to be alive because when you talk, you'll hear lots of echo. A modern movie theater has a dead, muffled sound because the walls, ceiling, and floor are covered with sound absorbing materials. A church auditorium is somewhere in-between.

➢ If you're in a gymnasium, talking loud doesn't really help because it increases the echo. Speak more slowly. Accentuate pronunciation.
➢ If the room is *dead*, speak as loudly as you can without distorting your voice. Stand up, turn and face the group directly, and keep your face up as you pray. If appropriate, walk to an elevated position directly in front of the group.

Now, back to leading a prayer during the worship service: let's say you've been asked to help collect the offering. You go forward at the appropriate time, the pastor asks everyone to bow their heads for the offertory prayer, then calls on you to lead it. Bam! There you stand with no time to prepare or even collect your thoughts. It really shouldn't be done this way, but there's a reason that it often is.

The ancestors of most American evangelicals were pioneers, independent folks that conquered and rebuilt this continent. You're not too far removed from them, and they were not far removed from the reformers that broke away from the liturgies of the European state religions. One of their core values was that any Christian could say a spontaneous prayer at any time. They didn't need a prayer book, priest, or even a preacher to pray. "I can do it myself, thank you."

So there you are, a proud descendant of your pioneering forefathers, and modern-day example of the priesthood of the believer. But what do you say? A good rule of thumb for this kind of prayer is to think of it as a 'blessing'. You're probably expected to ask God's blessing on some person or thing. Offertory prayers are a blessing on the offering and thanksgiving for God's provision. In a benediction prayer, you're asking God's blessing on the congregation as they disperse back into the world.

These kinds of prayers should be brief because people have a very short attention span when they are still with their eyes closed.

Preparation:

➢ Ask the congregation to bow their heads, assuming the worship leader hasn't already done so. If he has, your preparation time is reduced to about two seconds.
➢ Imagine yourself on your knees in the throne room of God with the congregation on their knees behind you.
➢ Ask yourself, *Why are we here?*

Salutation:

➢ Begin the prayer with, "Dear Heavenly Father…" If you're still trying to get your thoughts together, it's okay to hesitate for a few seconds here.
➢ Give honor to God with praise or thanksgiving for something related to the situation for which you've been asked to pray.

Petition:

➢ Get quickly to the heart of the matter. Whatever was on your heart when you asked the question, *why are we here*, becomes the focus of your petition to God.
➢ Pray about church needs, especially if they have been mentioned during the service and this is the first prayer since they were mentioned.
➢ Keep this prayer brief and to the point. After thirty seconds to a minute, the congregation will be drifting away mentally.

Benediction:

➢ A Biblical benediction is often appropriate during a worship service. See chapter 5.
➢ Support the traditions of the congregation. For instance, if your church always uses the Lord's Prayer as a benediction to the offertory prayer, it's not your place to change that.
➢ Conclude with, "In Jesus' name we pray, amen." if there's no tradition to follow and you don't feel that a Biblical benediction is appropriate.

STUDY GUIDE:

1. Should you talk directly into the side or the top of a microphone? _____

2. Most of these prayers can be considered a _____ on some person or thing.

Discussion question: What do our pioneer ancestors have to do with the way we lead prayer in our worship services?

Chapter 9

Saying a Prayer in Times of Tragedy

Disaster, Unexpected Death, etc.

The same things that make tragedies such a mine-field of spiritual and emotional malfunction also provide the greatest opportunities to become a channel of the life-giving grace of Jesus.

For many pastors, it's the moment they fear most, and it's so frightening, many laymen simply will not do it. Praying with someone who's just experienced a tragedy is truly a daunting responsibility. Whether it's the parent whose child has committed suicide or the spouse who's lost their mate in some sudden and terrible way, what do you say? Even more significantly, what do you pray?

Fear of making a foolish mistake in such emotion-packed circumstances isn't a bad thing. Stupid and even hurtful things are sometimes said under these conditions and people tend to remember them a long time.

Now consider this. The same things that make tragedies such a mine-field of spiritual and emotional malfunction also provide the greatest opportunities to become a channel of the life-giving grace of Jesus. Here are four truths that will help you pray lovingly and effectively in these most difficult situations:

1. You are not God.

➢ If they're asking the question, "Why did God let this happen?" don't try to answer it. Even if you knew the answer, they're not emotionally ready to deal with it.
➢ If they're angry at God, that's His problem. Instead of trying to defend Him, be a channel of His love for them, which could be the beginning of healing.

2. You are not their judge.

➢ Pray for them regardless of their spiritual condition. Tragedies happen to good and bad people, Christians and non-Christians. You can pray for them all.
➢ Remind yourself that from God's point of view, you're not as righteous as you

think and they're not as bad as you've heard. Keep in mind that many people make their turn toward Christ after experiencing the love of God through a non-judgmental, kind, caring Christian who ministers to them in a time of tragedy.

3. You are not their counselor.

➢ Friends and helpers are much more appreciated in times of tragedy than counselors so unless asked, leave the advice giving to someone else.

4. You are a New Testament priest.

➢ Help them get in contact with God at a time when they're not sure they can or even want to.
➢ Always ask, "How can I pray for you?" Listen to their answer carefully. The needs they express may be very different than you expect.
➢ Pray *for* them in two ways.
   a. First, voice *their* prayer *for* them. Pray what they want to say to God. Whatever they said when you asked them, "How can I pray for you?" pray for that as specifically as you can.
   b. Then, voice *your* prayer *for* them. Let them hear your personal conversation with the Heavenly Father about their needs.

With those truths in mind, you can approach this critical prayer opportunity with the same progression you've used in previous situations.

Preparation:

➢ Pray about their need before you visit them. Seek God's heart for these people and their situation.
➢ Situate yourself so they can hear you.
➢ Ask that distractions, like a loud TV, be turned down.
➢ Express your feelings and condolences for the tragedy they've experienced.
➢ Ask if they would like for you to pray. By saying yes, they join the prayer.
➢ Ask them if there's anything specifically they would like you to pray for.
➢ Listen. Try to hear their heart-cry. Don't analyze them. Make a mental list of the needs they mention.
➢ Ask those nearby to bow with you for prayer or at least announce to them that you are going to have prayer.
➢ Imagine yourself before God with these people gathered around you.

Salutation:

➢ Begin the prayer with, "Dear Heavenly Father…"
➢ Give honor to God. Never is it more important to acknowledge that He is God and you, with those around you, are in desperate need of His help.

Petition:

➢ Get quickly to the heart of the matter because this usually needs to be a brief prayer.
➢ Ask God for exactly what they requested earlier. If you don't think it's a particularly appropriate request, let God decide. In those situations, I pray

like this, "Lord, my friend feels that…and wants you to…"

➤ Pray your heart – humbly, honestly, powerfully. If your heart's broken, pray it. If your mind is confused, pray it.

➤ Pray specifically. If you've seen things that they need God to do, even if they didn't request it, pray for it as specifically as you can, but don't preach. For instance, it would be good to pray, "Dear God, please help these young children through this difficult time." It would be more specific to pray, "Lord, it breaks my heart to think about _____ having to explain all this to these precious children. Please give her/him the words to say and the right time to say them."

➤ Ask if someone else would like to voice a prayer, if appropriate. In some situations, it can become a sweet time of loving intercession.

Benediction:

➤ Quoting a short scripture like Isaiah 53:4a is very appropriate. You could say something like this, "Father, in your word it says, 'Surely He has borne our griefs and carried our sorrows.' Thank you for your help."

"In Jesus' name, amen."

STUDY GUIDE:

1. You are not _____, their _____, or their _____, but you are a _____.

2. You should always ask them, "How can I pray for you?" True or False

3. _____. Try to hear their heart-cry. Don't _____ them.

4. It's OK to ask for a TV or other distraction to be turned down. True or False

Discussion question: Explain the two ways you can pray 'for' a person in a time of tragedy.

PRAYER GUIDE by Lowell Snow

Chapter 10

Leading a Round-Robin Prayer Time

Bible Study Class, Retreats, Prayer Ministry Groups, etc.

This method is effective when time is limited or the group isn't prepared for more complicated techniques.

Round-robin prayer is perhaps the simplest and most often used form of group prayer. It involves a group of people praying monologue prayers, one after the other, often around a circle. The idea is that the group prays silently, in harmony with each person who prays out loud.

This method is effective when time is limited or the group isn't prepared for more complicated techniques. In either case, as prayer leader, you'll decide on a way to lead that fits your situation and facilitate the prayer time so that members of the group can participate freely.

In some situations, you'll need to receive prayer requests before the prayer time begins. If you expect this to be the case; study chapter 15. It will help you determine whether prayer requests are needed and how to handle them.

In any round-robin prayer situation, you'll want to designate who'll begin and end the prayer time before it starts. It's best to begin the prayer time yourself unless there's a compelling reason for someone else to do it. I often begin and end it myself simply because it eliminates any confusion.

Here are several ways of leading a round-robin prayer time.

➢ **Random volunteer prayers** – This is the most common method and will work well in most church situations. If you're asked to lead a group prayer with no opportunity to prepare, this will be the method to use. Tell them that you'll say the first prayer followed by anyone who wants to pray out loud. Tell them that you'll conclude the prayer time as well.

➢ **Volunteer prayers for specific requests** - This whole process can be done as one continuous prayer. To accomplish this, simply tell them to remain with their heads bowed between each request. It's also helpful to ask them to refrain from saying 'amen' at the conclusion of their individual prayers. After saying the opening prayer; state a specific request and ask for a volunteer to say a prayer for that need. Then proceed to the next request, asking for another volunteer to pray. For some requests, it may be appropriate to ask for two or three volunteers.

> **Pray in order** – This works best in a group where most of the group are willing to pray out loud. Ask someone to say the first prayer, followed by each person to their left or right. Make it clear that a person who doesn't want to pray out loud can simply remain silent so the next person will know to continue. The prayer time will conclude when everyone in the circle has had opportunity to pray.

> **Pray in order while holding hands in a circle** – This is similar to the previous method, but works well in larger groups and groups where many do not want to pray out loud. Have the group stand or sit in a circle and join hands. Tell them that you will pray first then squeeze the hand of the person next to you. If this person doesn't want to pray out loud, all they have to do is squeeze the hand of the next person. You'll conclude the prayer time when the prayer and 'squeezed hands' go all the way around the circle and back to you.

By far, the most common situation in which you might lead a round-robin prayer is at the beginning or end of a Bible study class, but other situations will use the same principles. You should have no problem adapting the following progression to any situation where round-robin prayer is appropriate.

The following suggestions assume that you're just getting started as a prayer guide. After you've led this type of group prayer a few times, you'll be able to do it with little or no preparation.

Preparation:

Before the meeting checklist:

☐ Ask the Lord for insight. As soon as you know that you'll be leading a group prayer situation, start praying about it during your personal devotions.

☐ Consider the prayer requests issue and read chapter 15. Make preparations as needed.

☐ Consider which method of round-robin prayer will work best for you and your group. Study that method and, if you're nervous; find a quiet place to practice.

When it's time to pray:

> Receive prayer requests if appropriate.
> Explain to the group how you're going to lead the prayer time.
> Identify who will say the first and last prayer.
> Ask the group to bow their heads for prayer.
> Think of yourself in the throne room of God with this group on their knees beside you, as they quiet down.

Salutation:

> Begin the opening prayer with the salutation of your choice, such as, "Dear Heavenly Father." If someone else is leading the opening prayer, ask them to pray now.
> Continue with praise and honor to the Lord.

Petition:

➢ Confess the group's need for the Lord's forgiveness and grace. Ask His blessing and protection over the prayer time.

➢ Conclude your prayer without saying amen. A common practice in group prayer is simply to say, "In Jesus' name." This signals that you've concluded, but expect someone else to continue the prayer.

➢ Prompt the group as needed. Don't be afraid to speak up with further instructions or encouragement if they're having a hard time following your instructions.

Benediction:

➢ Ask someone to say the concluding prayer. If you're leading this prayer, give praise and thanksgiving to the Lord for His attention to the group's prayers. Use the benediction of your choice.

➢ Conclude the benediction with 'amen' so the group will understand that the prayer time has concluded.

STUDY GUIDE:

1. In round-robin prayer, members of the group pray _____ prayers, one after the other, often around a _____.

2. It's a good idea to designate who'll begin and end the prayer time. True or False

3. If you're nervous about leading a prayer, it's good to find a quiet place and _____.

Discussion question: Why do you think the round-robin form of group prayer is the most often used?

Part Three

Prayer Guide Techniques

ach one should use whatever gift he has received to serve others, faithfully administering God's grace in its various forms. If anyone speaks, he should do it as one speaking the very words of God. If anyone serves, he should do it with the strength God provides, so that in all things God may be praised through Jesus Christ. To him be the glory and the power for ever and ever. Amen. 1 Peter 4:10-11 (NIV)

Prepare for the Challenge

Most people will never climb a mountain because they're afraid, aren't physically fit, or just don't see the point. Most Christians will never become prayer warriors because they're afraid, aren't spiritually fit, or just don't see the point.

The tallest mountain I ever climbed was 12,000 feet in elevation and had a clearly marked trail all the way to the top. All I had to do was follow the signs and walk. Climbing that mountain was just an extension of things I do all the time. The group prayer of most Christians is a little like that, just an extension of the monologue prayers they experience regularly.

If I wanted to climb a real mountain of say 25,000 feet, I'd need a guide. The guide would teach me skills I know nothing of, engage me in strengthening exercises so I could endure conditions I've never experienced, and would guide me along a path more difficult than any I've ever walked.

If Christian groups are to actually encounter God in prayer, they need a guide. They need someone who'll not be satisfied with business as usual and knows how to motivate and lead them to meet God more intimately.

The prayer guide techniques are not just an extended version of what you've always done. The way of the prayer guide is a different way. It doesn't tell people to pray more or pray harder, it guides them into an encounter with God.

That sounds great doesn't it? It's exactly what you want for your group, but a little warning may be appropriate at this point. Not everyone wants to encounter God. Some are very satisfied with monologue prayer that does more to make them feel good about themselves than actually communicate with God. Why? Because

we all have a natural fear of God when we actually get close to Him.

Read the following passage several times, trying to experience the situation with all of your senses. Imagine how it would have looked, sounded, smelled, felt, and even tasted to be in that group at the foot of Mt. Sinai.

> All the people saw the lightning and the smoke billowing from the mountain, and heard the thunder and the long, frightening trumpet blast; and they stood at a distance, shaking with fear.
> They said to Moses, "You tell us what God says and we will obey, but don't let God speak directly to us, or it will kill us."
> "Don't be afraid," Moses told them, "for God has come in this way to show you his awesome power, so that from now on you will be afraid to sin against him!"
> As the people stood in the distance, Moses entered into the deep darkness where God was.
> Exodus 20:18-21 TLB

Why are these people so frightened? Why isn't Moses?

Moses indicates that sin was the source of their fear. These people still had much of the pagan Egyptian culture in them. In fact, many were only there to get away from slavery and had no real intention of becoming followers of Moses' God. That's why they would so quickly worship the golden calf not long after this awesome experience. Moses, on the other hand,

PRAYER GUIDE by Lowell Snow

had put his life on the line to be obedient to God and had been living a righteous life for many years.

Also, the people were not accustomed to being close to God and Moses was. They were satisfied with religious rituals that helped them feel better about themselves while Moses had a conversational relationship with the Almighty.

Some in your group may have unconfessed sin in their lives or may not even be true followers of Christ. Being led into God's presence will make these people uncomfortable. They are likely to react like the Hebrews in the passage above.

Others of your group have been faithful followers of Christ for many years and become satisfied with things as they are. These folks may present your most difficult challenge because they have good reasons for doing prayer the way they always have. When you introduce something new, they have to decide if it's OK.

Have you ever heard the adage, 'When in doubt, leave it out'? The logic will go like this, "If it was OK to pray this way we would have been doing it this way before, but we haven't done it this way before so there must be something wrong with it."

How do you deal with criticism? Do you get your feelings hurt, get angry, become defensive, or quit? None of these are appropriate for the prayer guide. You're embarking on a pilgrimage of guiding people into situations and experiences they've not had before. You must be prepared to answer their questions and deal positively with their criticisms.

The truth is, that old adage about leaving it out if you have a doubt, is not necessarily bad. Your goal is not to bulldoze over their doubts, but to eliminate their doubt. To that end, in the chapters ahead, you'll not only be instructed in how to use a particular technique, but how to defend its value with a Biblical foundation.

I once led a special prayer time in a large church and received many words of appreciation afterwards. A couple of weeks later I received a long e-mail from a church member who had read a lot about the influence of paganism on Christianity. He was concerned that my visualization technique was spiritually dangerous. He had expressed this opinion to others in the church and therefore felt that he should express it to me also.

I returned his e-mail, saying that he had every right to express his opinion to anyone he wanted and thanked him for giving me the opportunity to respond. Then I presented the theology behind the techniques that I had used. He responded quickly and it seemed that I had been removed from his heretic list.

My point is that you can't please everyone all the time, and sometimes people will completely misunderstand what you're doing. In those situations, remember that a soft answer turns away anger and a good explanation can sometimes alleviate confusion.

Introducing new techniques:

Don't try to learn all the techniques at once. The techniques of prayer by suggestion in chapter 11, topical praying in chapter 12, scriptural meditation in chapter 13, and Biblical visualization in chapter 14; are presented in the order I think they are easiest to learn and introduce. When you get to the chapters in Part IV, you'll find that the techniques are actually used in a different order.

My suggestion is that you read the entire book so you have an understanding of where you're headed as a prayer guide. Then come back and study chapter 11 on prayer by suggestion. Start using it and when you're comfortable with it, move on to the next, and so on.

Before you introduce any technique to the group: study it, plan it, practice it, and believe in it.

Study the material. After re-reading the chapter on the particular technique you plan to introduce, move to Part IV of the book and find the chapter on the particular type of prayer group you're leading. It will give you specific instructions on how to implement the technique.

If you're still confused, ask a friend to read the material and discuss it with you. Remember, all of the techniques are used in those chapters, but you won't want to introduce them to your group all at once.

Plan the prayer time. Anything worth doing is worth doing well and anything worth doing well requires planning. Again, follow the instructions from Part IV that apply to your group.

Practice the technique. Find a private place where you can practice using the technique out loud. Go through your plan in real time. Make adjustments to the plan until you feel confident.

Believe in the value of what you're doing. If you're having doubts, talk it over with the Lord. Ask Him for confidence and faith. Re-read sections of this book that have motivated you. Remind yourself of why you're trying to become a prayer guide.

Don't give up. The pilgrimage of a prayer guide isn't finished in a week, or a month, or even a year. You'll always be reaching forward, upward.

STUDY GUIDE:

1. The way of the prayer guide is a _____ way. It doesn't tell people to pray _____ or pray _____, it guides them into an _____ with _____.

2. What was the real source of the Hebrew's fear when they saw God come down on Mt. Sinai: fear of fire, misunderstanding of Moses' instructions, or sin?

3. There are four things you should do before introducing a new prayer technique: _____ it, _____ it, _____ it, and _____ in it.

Discussion question: Why do you think some people might feel that it's inappropriate to plan and/or practice for leading prayer?

PRAYER GUIDE by Lowell Snow

Chapter 11

Prayer by Suggestion

The Tool of a Prayer Guide

Like the fishing guide who brings anglers to the best place to fish, the prayer guide is bringing his group into a spiritual position where they are most likely to have a personal encounter with God.

The most powerful group prayers in the New Testament contain this phrase; "with one accord". The first, in Acts 1:14, is the ten day prayer meeting preceding Pentecost and the other, at the onset of persecution in Acts 4:24. This second passage was the time God literally shook the foundations of the house where the disciples were praying for boldness.

How does a group of Christians pray that way? How can we get our minds all tuned-in and praying about the same thing at the same time?

The Acts 4 passage is included below in its entirety because it came at a critical point in Christian history and is a model of powerful group prayer. Peter and John had been put in jail overnight, threatened with severe punishment if they continued to preach about Jesus, then let go.

And being let go, they went to their own companions and reported all that the chief priests and elders had said to them. So when they heard that, they raised their voice to God with one accord and said: "Lord, You are God,

who made heaven and earth and the sea, and all that is in them, who by the mouth of Your servant David have said:

'Why did the nations rage, and the people plot vain things? The kings of the earth took their stand, and the rulers were gathered together against the LORD and against His Christ.' (from Psalms 2:1)

For truly against Your holy Servant Jesus, whom You anointed, both Herod and Pontius Pilate, with the Gentiles and the people of Israel, were gathered together to do whatever Your hand and Your purpose determined before to be done. Now, Lord, look on their threats, and grant to Your servants that with all boldness they may speak Your word, by stretching out Your hand to heal, and that signs and

wonders may be done through the
name of Your holy Servant
Jesus."

And when they had prayed, the
place where they were assembled
together was shaken; and they
were all filled with the Holy Spirit,
and they spoke the word of God
with boldness.

Acts 4:23-31 NKJV

Wow! What an example to Christians everywhere. These people were tuned-in and turned-on to God's will in their lives. Faced with persecution, they didn't pray for deliverance and prosperity, but boldness and power. Their prayer was specific, unified, included scripture, and revealed complete faith that God would answer. That's some powerful praying.

So back to our question; how does a group of Christians pray with one accord? As you read the scripture above, you may have assumed that Peter or John led this as a monologue prayer while everyone else listened. Look more closely at what it says; "...they raised their voice to God with one accord..."

It says 'they' raised their voice. If you read several translations you'll find that most actually translate the word 'voice' as 'voices' because 'they' refers to those who heard the story from Peter and John, not Peter or John.

So how'd they do that? How did all those people pray this rather complicated prayer together? Did they repeat it one line at a time the way our ancestors used to 'line-out' hymns before they could afford hymn books? Did they write it down then recite it together. Was it a memorized prayer they prayed together often? I can't give you a definite answer, but I do know they did it and God liked it a lot.

The prayer by suggestion technique that I'm going to teach you in this chapter may or may not have been used by first century Christians, but it is a technique that can be used in almost any

group prayer situation to guide people to pray in agreement. I can't guarantee that your group will be as in-tune with the Holy Spirit or as committed to Christ as those first disciples, but I do promise that your group will be drawn together in prayer by suggestion.

Have you ever been on a fishing trip with a guide? If so, you know that those guys are amazing outdoorsmen. They could catch ten times as many fish as you, but that's not their purpose. Their job is to help *you* catch fish. As a *prayer guide*, your job is to help the people in your group talk to God. You may be able to pray a better prayer than they, but that's not your purpose.

Leading prayer by suggestion is the most effective tool for getting an entire group to talk with God. This simple technique will lead your group, no matter the size, into an encounter with the Father. You'll actually become a prayer *guide* rather than a prayer *leader*.

Consider the average prayer meeting from the average Christian's point of view. This person loves God, but seldom if ever speaks in public. Most of their praying consists of simple prayers at bedtime, meals, etc. Their prayers are not spontaneous and generally vary little from day to day.

As they sit in a prayer meeting, they probably have no intention of praying out loud. As the more outgoing people begin to pray, they try to pay attention and agree with what's being said. That works for the first prayer, but then the prayers become long and monotonous. It's not that they don't care; but by the fifth or sixth prayer, they're bored and thinking about everything but the prayers being said. They may even be fighting to stay awake.

These are the folks you want to get involved in your group prayer. Forget about getting them to pray out loud. Leave that up to the Holy Spirit. Some of the greatest prayer warriors never pray in public. Their personalities are so meek that they just can't do it. You don't want to do anything that would make these precious people feel guilty or manipulated. Your job is to provide an atmosphere of prayer in which they'll feel free to participate as the Holy Spirit leads them. Prayer by suggestion is a way to guide them down that path.

Besides the meek, you'll also have people in your group that are struggling with issues too private to mention. Beginning the prayer time with prayer by suggestion gives them the opportunity to go to the Lord and get these concerns resolved so that they can participate in the rest of the prayer time.

Often, in a public prayer, you'll hear something like this, "Lord, help us with those problems that burden our hearts." The prayer leader then goes on with the rest of the prayer. That prayer leader has good intentions, but there are a couple of things amiss with this way of leading group prayer: It's not specific to the needs of the individual and it doesn't give God a chance to respond. Here's a better way:

Prayer by Suggestion

Consider how much each member of that group would benefit if they were *guided* in prayer with the following *suggestions*. "Now, as we continue our prayer, would you talk to the Lord silently, right now, about that issue in your life that's troubling you the most? God already knows about it, and wants to help you with it, but He's waiting right now for you to bring it to Him...trust His love, trust His mercy, trust His power." Then the group is given time to pray their own prayers silently. After an appropriate time, the prayer guide makes another suggestion, and so on.

Like the fishing guide who brings anglers to the best place to fish, this prayer guide is bringing his group into a spiritual position where they are most likely to have a personal encounter with God. The beauty of this way of leading prayer is its simplicity. Here's how you do it.

After you begin the prayer with just two or three sentences of salutation, start suggesting one thing at a time for the group to pray about. You'll make the suggestion out loud, and then give them

time to pray about it silently. Make it clear that you want them all to pray silently.

Instead of talking to God for them, you, as prayer guide, are guiding their prayer with your suggestions. The best way to know how long to wait between suggestions is to do what you've suggested, yourself. If you suggest that they pray for their pastor, then pray for your pastor silently as you give them time to do the same.

By leading prayer this way, the whole group is actually praying in agreement, whether they're led to pray about a common problem like the folks in Acts 4 or being guided to pray about personal issues as in the example above.

Have you ever listened to seventy thousand sports fans as they cheer their favorite team? It's an amazing sound isn't it? I was driving my family by a college football stadium one Saturday evening and we rolled down the windows to hear what was happening. The announcer was saying something over the public address system which we could hear clearly. Then something happened on the field and the crowd went wild! We later learned that it was a recovered fumble followed by a touchdown run. The roar from the crowd was so loud! It was really quite astonishing even outside the stadium.

My wife made the comment that it may be like that when God listens to the prayers of His people. He can hear the prayer of the one person announcing a public prayer for the group, but what really gets His attention is when they all pray at once. Even if they're praying silently, as their heart-cry goes up all at once, it must truly be a thrilling sound to the One who sits on the throne.

Like the fans who sit in the football stadium anxiously awaiting the next opportunity to cheer their team, God's people anxiously wait for an opportunity to talk with Him. All you have to do is give them the chance by guiding them along.

Of course you won't begin the prayer by suggesting the deepest issues of life, as in the illustration earlier. You'll begin with suggestions of praise, thanksgiving, repentance, etc. We'll discuss that in later chapters. You'll find an example of prayer by suggestion in the sample prayer in chapter 19.

Guiding prayer by suggestion is a simple yet effective form of group prayer, but you'll likely find it difficult to do. Why?

➢ You've never done it this way before.
➢ It involves silence.

The problem won't be with the people you're guiding. I've never had anyone complain about being lead to pray in this way, but prayer leaders seem to struggle with it.

The only constructive criticism I get from time to time about prayer by suggestion is that people feel rushed because the prayer guide doesn't give them enough time to pray for what's been suggested.

Don't be surprised if you feel panicky the first time you try it. Slow down, there's no need to rush. Remember to pray for what you've suggested yourself. This will help you keep the pace.

Even if you fail, don't give up. If you apply nothing else in this book, learn to guide prayer by suggestion. It's such a blessing to the majority of folks that are being left out of most group prayer. Please, for their sake, guide them to the throne.

STUDY GUIDE:

1. The value in prayer by suggestion is that it manipulates everyone into praying out loud even if they don't want to. True or False

2. When using prayer by suggestion, the leader _____ something for the group to pray about, and then waits while each member prays their own prayer _____.

3. The best way to know how long to wait between suggestions is to _____ _____ _____ _____.

Discussion question: How is being a prayer guide similar to being a fishing guide?

Chapter 12

Topical Praying

Conversational Prayer

"Praying conversationally makes prayer such a natural means of spiritual togetherness". Rosalind Rinker

My group prayer experience as a teen was greatly influenced by Rosalind Rinker's little book, *PRAYER - Conversing with God*.[3] In it, she said,

"Praying conversationally (that is, praying back and forth on a single subject until a new one is introduced by the Spirit) makes prayer such a natural means of 'spiritual togetherness' that the healing love of God touches us all as we are in His presence."

Praying topically, will:

- Keep the prayer moving,
- Involve more people,
- Unify the group to agree in prayer.

With topical praying, each person is encouraged to pray as often as they want, but to pray for one thing at a time. The group is instructed to continue to pray for the same topic

---

[3] *PRAYER - Conversing with God*, by Rosalind Rinker, Copyright 1959, published by Zondervan Publishing House, Grand Rapids Michigan, preface

until someone feels led to pray about another. The purpose is to give the group an opportunity to agree in prayer. Matthew 28:19-20 is the Great Commission. Matthew 18:19-20 is:

The Great Commission of Prayer

"Again, I tell you that if two of you on earth **agree** about anything you ask for, it will be done for you by my Father in heaven. For where two or three come together in my name, there am I with them." Matthew 18:19-20 (NIV)

Great power is available to a group of born-again followers of Christ, living righteous lives, who agree with each other and with God in prayer.

If you've been active in a church for any length of time, you know that evangelism and group prayer are the two hardest things to accomplish. Both are natural expressions of a genuine relationship with Christ, but hard to start and continue because Satan works tirelessly against them.

Here are four simple rules that you, as prayer guide, need to understand if you're to have an effective topical prayer group:

The Four Rules of Topical Prayer

1. **Each person prays a short prayer about one topic at a time.**

2. **Each person prays as often as they want.**

3. **The group continues praying about the same topic until someone introduces another topic.**

4. **Each topical prayer is part of the whole and doesn't need a benediction.**

Educate your group in topical praying before you begin the prayer time. You'll have to remind them of these principles often, even during the prayer time. If you don't, they'll go back to their old ways.

One prayer warrior shared with me that she had introduced her prayer ministry group to the principles of topical praying. Everyone was excited and felt that their prayer time was much better. However, when she returned from a two week absence, the group was praying exactly as they had before. Not being the actual leader of the group, she felt that her suggestion had been rejected. Perhaps, but probably the group just slipped back into doing what was familiar.

Leadership is the key. The regular prayer leader must be instructed in and committed to topical praying or it's not likely to continue.

My recommendation to someone who wants to introduce topical prayer to a group where they're not the leader is simply to start doing it themselves. Don't be afraid to pray multiple times, but pray short prayers about one topic.

Hopefully, the other members of the group will notice and ask questions.

If you are the prayer leader, as you begin to train your group in this new way of praying, the first and most important principle is to get them to pray for one topic at a time. This can be anything the Lord places on someone's heart. The point is to train the group to continue praying about that one topic until led to pray for another.

> Let's say that Sue voices this prayer, "Dear Lord, help my friend Kay who has pneumonia. The doctor says it's very serious."
>
> Across the room, Bill takes up the prayer, "Father, Kay is very frightened by this. She told me that she's afraid that it will eventually lead to her death. Please help us minister to her in a way that encourages her as she continues this battle."
>
> Sue prays again, "Lord, please encourage Kay as she goes to the doctor this week. I pray that she will get an encouraging word from him."
>
> A third group member prays, "Dear Jesus, we want to pray together that the infection in Kay's lungs will be completely healed. We know that you can do this and we believe together that you will. Thank you Lord Jesus."
>
> Now a fourth member of the group joins in, "Lord, we pray that right now Kay will feel your encouragement and we pray that you'll give some of us opportunities to visit and pray with her this week."
>
> Now there's a silence for several seconds, then someone leads the prayer in another direction, "Father, I'm very concerned about our pastor search committee. They seem very discouraged…"

Praying this way leads to real group prayer. Even those who are not praying out loud will stay tuned-in. It's worth the effort to guide your group into this kind of prayer.

One effective way to train people in topical praying is to take them on a prayer walk. (chapter 16) Prayer walking is topical prayer because it's so natural to pray this way when the group has their eyes open, praying for the needs that they're all looking at together.

A more practical way to train your group in topical prayer is to combine it with prayer by suggestion from chapter 11. Suggest a topic and ask the group to voluntarily pray out loud for just that one topic. After two or three have prayed about that, suggest another, and so on. After doing it this way for two or three prayer sessions, ask them to guide themselves by following the four rules of topical prayer. If they're still struggling with it, go back to guiding them for a couple more sessions.

Some of your group may never get it. They're so entrenched in their prayer speeches that they just can't break out of that mold. Remember, they're not bound before God to follow your lead. Just keep explaining the principles before each prayer session and pray for them to see the light. If they never get it, don't worry. Most of the group will.

———————————————

There's a problem that can arise in any prayer session but it's a particular hindrance to topical prayer - some people talk too much, even when they're talking to God. They may be very sincere, but their long rambling prayers can kill a wonderful prayer time. If, after hearing the principles of topical prayer in several prayer sessions, they continue to pray this way, you might ask them to lead an opening or closing prayer. At least this will move their long prayer out of the main prayer time.

Don't make a battle out of this. There are some issues in the family of God that we just live with or work around. I love the old story about the young pastor who visited a saintly deacon one morning after a particularly frustrating meeting the night before. The old deacon asked the young pastor to walk with him across one of his fields. As they walked the discouraged young man expressed his frustration and anger about one particularly stubborn church member.

The wise old farmer stopped and shoved his toe into the freshly plowed soil. "This here's fine soil now, but when I bought this place, there was a big stump right here."

"I bet you blew it out with dynamite, didn't you?" the young preacher said.

"I tried that and nearly killed myself. Then I dug and hacked away for days, but never made much progress. As time went by, I learned to just plow around it."

"I think I see your point, but what happened to it. How'd you finally get it out?"

"Never did." said the old deacon. "Every year it got a little smaller and every year I plowed a little closer."

———————————————

If you wait for the perfect circumstance, you'll never do anything. Make a commitment to guiding prayer effectively. Don't give up just because the first few times don't go as you hoped. Many great ideas are dropped just before they take hold. Stick with it.

STUDY GUIDE:

1. The purpose of topical prayer is to give the group an opportunity to _____ in prayer.

2. The Great Commission is found in Matthew 28:19-20. The great commission of prayer is found in Matthew _____:19-20.

3. As you begin to train your group in this new way of praying, the first and most important principle is to get them to pray for one _____ at a time.

4. A practical way to train your group in topical prayer is to combine it with prayer by _____.

Discussion question: What similarities do you see between topical prayer and casual conversation between friends?

Chapter 13

Scriptural Meditation

The Meditation of My Heart...

The purpose of Biblical Meditation is to get the group's attention and focus it on the Lord or a Biblical truth.

May the words of my mouth and the meditation of my heart be pleasing in your sight, O LORD, my Rock and my Redeemer. Psalms 19:14 (NIV)

You've gotten your group together. They're in the same place physically, but how do you get them in the same place mentally and spiritually so that they'll be ready to pray in agreement? Scriptural meditation.

The Bible speaks of meditating about many things:

➤ God (Mal. 3:16)
➤ The love of God (Ps. 48:9)
➤ The laws of God (Ps.119:97)
➤ The precepts of God (Ps. 119:27)
➤ The things that God has done for you in the past (Ps. 143:5)
➤ The good things you have been taught by godly teachers (I Tim. 4:15)
➤ The Word of God (Joshua 1:8)

For our purposes, we'll talk exclusively about meditating on the Word of God.

The term *meditation* has gotten a bad rap because it's so closely tied to Eastern religions and the humanistic New Age movement. Let me assure you that you're not going to have your prayer group sitting cross-legged on the floor and humming Amazing Grace as a mantra.

However, Christianity did start in the Middle East and meditation has always been part of its practice. Our European ancestors westernized it, but we still do it.

Have you ever heard the term ruminate? That's a good western word with a Latin heritage. What does it mean? For cows, it means chewing their cud. For people, it means to turn a matter over and over in the mind, ponder, *meditate*.

Do you ever say, "I'm going to have to think about that." or, "I need to pray about that before I make a decision."? Sounds like a western version of meditation to me.

Well, I hope you get my point; meditation is part of our day to day lives. We don't practice it in the transcendental meditation form, but we meditate about things all the time and it can help the members of your group direct their attention to the things of God as you begin your prayer time. Here's why it's important.

The people in your group are distracted by a thousand things. If you start praying without first getting their attention, you've already lost most of them. The purpose of Biblical meditation is to get the group's attention and focus it on the Lord or a Biblical truth.

If you're uncomfortable with the term meditation or you think it will be a hindrance to some in your group, don't worry, it's not important to use the term. Just ask them to *think about* or *listen to* the scripture.

One reason meditation works so well is that it works toward the positive side of thought. As you begin a prayer time, you won't say, "OK, stop thinking about all your problems and think about this scripture." They'd never hear the first word of scripture because you inadvertently caused them to think about their problems. Always start by giving them a positive thing to do, like this, "As we prepare to talk with our Heavenly Father, please bow your heads and listen to the words of this scripture."

Note: If you're in a worship situation and the worship leader has already brought the group into the presence of the Lord through praise songs and perhaps even scripture songs, scriptural meditation may be redundant and should not be used. However, in that situation, be sure that there's no dead time between the end of the songs and the beginning of the prayer. See Appendix 1 for guidance.

In your preparation, locate a scripture that goes with the purpose of the prayer session you'll be leading. It doesn't need to be familiar, but it should be:

➢ Easy to read out loud
➢ Easily understood without explanation

Here are some examples:

If my people, who are called by my name, will humble themselves and pray and seek my face and turn from their wicked ways, then will I hear from heaven and will forgive their sin and will heal their land.
2 Chronicles 7:14 (NIV)

Pray all the time. Ask God for anything in line with the Holy Spirit's wishes. Plead with him, reminding him of your needs, and keep praying earnestly for all Christians everywhere.
Ephesians 6:18 (TLB)

Be joyful always; pray continually; give thanks in all circumstances, for this is God's will for you in Christ Jesus.
1Thessalonians 5:16-18 (NIV)

When you find a scripture that feels right, look it up in several translations and use the one that's easy to read and understand. (If your group has strong feelings about using a certain translation of the Bible, use the one they're comfortable with.) Read the verse out loud, over and over, until you're confident with it. Try to imagine that you're in a group listening to the words.

Read it slowly using different inflections and emphasizing different words and phrases. This is the way you'll want to read it to the group. By reading it differently each time, you can read it two or three times without losing their attention.

You'll find a good example of scriptural meditation in chapter 19, under the preparation section, at the beginning of the sample prayer.

STUDY GUIDE:

1. List three things the Bible says we should meditate on. _____ _____

   _____

2. Using scriptural meditation to focus the group's attention is important because they are

   _____.

3. Meditation works so well because it works toward the _____ _____ of thought.

4. The scriptures you use for scriptural meditation should be long and complicated so the group will

   have to really concentrate to understand them. True or False

Discussion question: Why do you think the author says to use only scripture as the object of meditation in preparation for prayer?

PRAYER GUIDE by Lowell Snow

Chapter 14

Biblical Visualization

Worth More Than a 1,000 Words

We are people of the faith. Those who **see** what others do not.

Few things focus attention better than a picture. By placing a Biblical image in the minds of those you're leading, you'll not only hold their attention, they'll be drawn together in one spiritual place.

Like meditation, visualization has gotten a bad name by associations with other religions and questionable mind over matter philosophies. Like meditation, it's a Biblical part of our faith that should not be rejected because of its misuse by others.

Visualization is part of faith.

If you were asked to prepare a Biblical definition of faith, you would almost certainly include the following passages;

Now faith is the substance of things hoped for, the evidence of things not seen. For by it the elders obtained a good testimony.
By faith we understand that the worlds were framed by the word of God, so that the things which are seen were not made of things which are visible.
Hebrews 11:1-3 (NKJV)

So Jesus said to them, "...if you have faith as a mustard seed, you will say to this mountain, 'Move from here to there,' and it will move; and nothing will be impossible for you.
Matthew 17:20 (NKJV)

Do you see the visualization theme in the Biblical concept of faith? It involves *seeing* what can't be seen or does not yet exist.

What's at the top of your personal prayer list right now? When you talk to God about it, what's in your mind's eye? More importantly, what's in your spirit's eye? If you have the faith of a mustard seed, you see it as God sees it in the future, not as it is right now. That's faith.

Seeing with our minds and spirits that which we can't see with our eyes is at the core of who and what we are as Christians. More than people of the Word, more than people of the church, more than anything: we are people of the faith. Those who **see** what others do not.

Jesus, the master of visualization

Jesus seldom taught without giving his disciples a mental picture. They're called parables. What comes to your mind when you read the words, *love your neighbor*? Do you not instantly see the Good Samaritan?

Why did Jesus use this visual form of teaching? Because, being the Creator, He knows that our brains are picture-oriented. It's the way we think.

Consider the word *cow*. Can you comprehend the word without having a picture of a cow in your mind?

You can't do it can you? That's because you think with pictures - and it's not just nouns. Try the same experiment with red cow, or big cow, or even invisible cow.

This is why visualization is one of the most powerful tools available for capturing the minds of human beings, so don't let the false religions have a monopoly on it. Let's learn to use it responsibly and Biblically.

As you prepare to use visualization in a particular group prayer setting, you'll search for a Biblical place or situation that could help your group prepare for prayer. For instance,

➢ If you're leading the prayer time at the beginning of a Bible study, you might ask the group to imagine themselves sitting on the hillside by the Sea of Galilee where Jesus is teaching and feeding the five thousand. (Matthew 14:13-21)
➢ If you're leading the prayer time at the conclusion of a Bible study, you would certainly want to consider using a situation from the passage or topic the group has just studied.
➢ If you're leading a prayer meeting where much of the time will be given to praying for the sick, you might ask the group to see themselves as the men who are tearing away the roof and letting their friend down

into a crowded house to be healed by Jesus. (Mark 2)
➢ If you're leading a group that will be praying about some problem, you might suggest that they see themselves in the sinking boat as Jesus comes walking on the water. (Matthew 14:22)

By using visualizations that connect with the subject of the prayer time to follow, you'll be using mental pictures in much the same way Jesus used parables to connect with the minds of His disciples.

Other Biblical visualizations that will work with most group prayer times are:

➢ The throne room of Heaven (Revelation 4:1-6)
➢ The Shekinah glory of God in the holy of holies (Leviticus 16:2, 2 Chronicles 3:8-14)
➢ The hillside where Jesus preached the Sermon on the Mount (Matthew 5:1)
➢ The upper-room where Jesus prayed for His apostles the night before His crucifixion (Luke 22:10-14)
➢ The Garden of Gethsemane (John 18:1-2)

At the conclusion of a church conference where emotions had run high and hurtful things said, I began the closing prayer like this, "As we bow for prayer, I want you to remember the first Passover in the Old Testament. To protect their families from the Death Angel, the head of each household spread the blood of a sacrificial lamb on the doorjamb of the entrance to his house. As we come to this time of prayer, I want you to imagine yourself going out your front door, dipping the brush in the bowl of blood, and painting it onto the molding around your front door. Now, as you finish, you turn around and see others, up and down the street, doing the same. There's your pastor. There's a church leader. And down the street, I want you to see that person you're most angry with. Just like you, the blood of the lamb is their only hope."

The next week, a leader in that church told me of a conversation he had with a deacon who'd been particularly aggravated with someone. He'd been struggling with these feelings for weeks, but when he *saw* that person putting the blood of the lamb on their doorpost, those angry feelings vanished.

On another occasion, the pastor of a large church that was going through some difficult times, asked me to lead the prayer time during the morning service. Shortly before I was to lead this prayer, the children's choir sang so I began the prayer time something like this, "Your pastor is coming to the altar for this special time of prayer, I want as many of you as can to come join him on your knees. As you come, remember how Jesus loved the children and taught us that we must come to God with the faith and attitude of a child." (Matthew 19:13-14)

I continued with a few more words along those lines until the people were settled in the altar area. Then I said, "Please bow your heads and imagine yourself as child, climbing up on the lap of Jesus. What does the child in you want to say to Jesus? Begin your conversation with God this morning with those words. Tell Him what your heart feels as you sit in the lap of your Savior." After ten or fifteen seconds of silence, I continued to guide them using prayer by suggestion, but several people later said that it was the visualization about the children that really helped them get past their adult struggles and back to the heart of their relationship with Jesus.

Do you see how a Biblical picture can bring a group, no matter the size, into an attitude of prayer? It's not actually part of the prayer, but it prepares them to pray. It helps them get their mind and spirit focused on the same thing.

Of the four group prayer techniques, this will be the most difficult for some, because it requires a degree of story telling ability. If you're one of those folks who can't tell a good story,

you'll have to work at using Biblical visualization. Don't be deterred though. Even if you have to learn the other techniques first and come back to this later, please do so, it's worth the effort.

Get started by using some of the examples in chapters 16 - 20 where you'll also receive specific instructions on developing, practicing, and using visualizations. Then, when you get a feel for it, you'll start coming up with your own. Here are some principles to follow:

➤ Stick with Biblical visualizations. They're less likely to have secondary meanings.
➤ Use Biblical situations that are familiar to most people.
➤ Use the second person, 'you'. This helps every person in the group see themselves in that situation.
➤ Don't drag it out or give so many details that they lose focus on the central theme of the mental picture.

Ideas for visualizations should usually start in your own memory of scripture because they need to be familiar. However, you should also study the passage that contains the situation you plan to use. The pictures you paint in people's minds will stay with them a long time so you want to get it right.

Use whatever resources are available to you. Try your church library. Many public libraries have good Bible study resources too. A good Bible study computer program can be very helpful. If you have a good internet connection, there are many resources there.

Generally, you'll find Bible encyclopedias and dictionaries more helpful for visualization than commentaries. Also look for picture books of the Holy Land. If you've been looking for a good reason to go on a tour to Israel, here it is. There's nothing like seeing it for yourself.

STUDY GUIDE:

1. There is a visualization theme in the Biblical concept of _____.

2. Jesus used a form of visualization in His _____.

3. Jesus knew that our brains are _____ oriented.

4. A good story telling ability is helpful in using Biblical visualization. True or False

Discussion question: What do you think the author means when he says that Biblical visualization helps people get their mind and spirit focused on the same thing? Why do you think that is important?

Chapter 15

Prayer Requests

Keeping the Main Thing the Main Thing

People have much more experience talking than praying.

People have much more experience talking than praying, so in many prayer meetings, discussion of prayer requests eats up most of the time. There's a difference of opinion on how best to deal with this issue.

➢ Some say to eliminate it all together by not having any prayer requests. These folks would say that the purpose of a prayer meeting is to present requests to God, not each other. (see the boxed prayer in chapter 12)

➢ Others feel that prayer requests are actually a form of prayer. They feel that during the request time, people who are too timid to pray out loud, voice their concerns in an attitude of faith.

In deciding how to lead your group, two factors will affect what you do: the purpose of the meeting and the personality of the group.

➢ If you're leading the **weekly meeting of your prayer ministry** team in which

you're given a printed list of prayer needs, you'll obviously need to go over that list. However, because this group is made up of experienced prayer warriors who meet together regularly, you should streamline this process so that it doesn't use up the prayer time.

➢ In a **home prayer meeting**, you may have just the opposite situation, no printed list of needs and some people who are reluctant to pray out loud. In this situation, a time of requests may be very helpful preparation.

  o The truth is, in many Bible study and prayer groups, the unstated, but primary purpose of the group is sharing. Eliminating prayer requests in such a group would be a mistake.

➢ If you lead a **small group of friends** who meet regularly to pray, you may find it very liberating to eliminate the request time and go straight to the Lord. Using the principles of topical prayer, each person will present their request to God.

When prayer requests are needed, here are several options to consider.

Prayer list prepared ahead of time:

➤ If you can anticipate most of the prayer requests, prepare a list ahead of time; and if it's long, make copies for everyone.

➤ If your group is Internet savvy, set up a blog or group where members can enter their requests between sessions. Then, when it's time for the meeting, you can print copies for everyone.

Written requests during the session:

➤ If you're leading a prayer time at the conclusion of a meeting or Bible Study, ask the leader if you may circulate a notepad during the meeting for folks to write their requests on.

o When they're through, if there's a copy machine available, slip out and make copies. (Many homes now have a scanner or printer that doubles as a copier.)

o This list can be used during the prayer time and during the members' private devotions during the week.

Note: Especially in small intimate groups, people can be very open and sometimes not very discrete about their requests. If these kinds of needs are written down, then copied, the potential for embarrassment and hurt feelings is evident. Be sure extra copies are not left lying around the meeting room.

o If there's no copier, you'll just have to read the list to them at the beginning of the prayer time.

✓ Tell the group that you want to keep the prayer request time to a minimum so the time in prayer can be maximized.

✓ Read through the list without comment or have them read over it silently. (If you start commenting on everything, everyone else will follow your example.)

✓ Ask if there are any additions or corrections. Write them on your copy of the list.

Oral requests at the beginning of the prayer time:

➤ Remind the group of the purpose of the prayer time and suggest that they wait and present their prayer requests directly to the Lord, unless there are details that need to be explained to the group.

➤ Take notes as they make requests.

➤ Look at your list toward the end of the prayer time, to be sure all requests have been prayed for.

Requests and the Prayer Ministry:

A prayer ministry must be much more attentive to its list of requests than other groups that pray together. Many authors have written volumes on this subject so I'll just touch on it.

➤ A prayer ministry should maintain contact information for those on their list so encouraging post cards and/or short phone calls can be made.

➤ A prayer ministry should maintain two lists:

o The full list - includes all the details of each request, who presented the request, the date of the initial request, dates of subsequent updates, and contact information. This list is confidential and only available to the church staff and prayer ministry team.

o The 'filtered' list - printed weekly for the whole congregation. It focuses on current needs that the congregation identifies with, usually not more than 15 or 20. It does not include embarrassing details and has a balance of Kingdom needs and temporal.

Handling prayer requests can be a challenge, but there are two related issues that we must also consider, gossip and people who talk too much.

Dealing with Gossip:

Often, there's a very fine line between genuine prayer requests and gossip. You, as prayer guide, must recognize that line for your group.

I was pastor in a rural community where everybody knew everybody and most were related. Because of these extensive interfamily relations, the requests segment of our mid-week prayer meetings were quite interesting at times.

Sometimes we would hear the following request, "We need to pray for _____ and _____, they're having trouble." Nobody had to ask what that meant. It was prayer request code for marriage problems.

In our situation, this seldom constituted gossip because everyone already knew about it. It does, however, illustrate the potential for gossip inherent in prayer requests.

As leader, you need to have a clear understanding of what gossip is. Here are some things that should be red flags anytime you hear them:

➤ A prayer request that includes information of a personal nature
➤ A prayer request that includes embarrassing information about a person not present
➤ A prayer request that includes embarrassing information about a person who hasn't requested prayer by the group

➤ A prayer request that includes derogatory accusations about someone who has allegedly done some wrong to the person being prayed for
➤ A prayer request that isn't a request for prayer, but further *information* about a troubled person for whom prayer has already been requested

These are just red warning flags. You'll have to decide if your group is crossing the line. If so, suggest the following guidelines:

➤ Prayer requests must be based on information that is factual and verifiable.
➤ Prayer requests must not include embarrassing information about people unless they have specifically asked that the information be presented to the group for prayer.

The power of your group's prayer has very much to do with their righteousness and little to do with how well informed they are about the person for whom they're praying. That being the case, it behooves us to be very careful not to slip into the sin of gossip.

Remind your group of the following verse:

…your Father knows the things you have need of before you ask Him.
Matthew 6:8b (NKJV)

Since God already knows all about every situation, getting all the juicy details of someone's misfortune or failure serves no purpose and has no place in a prayer meeting.

Dealing with someone who talks too much:

Talking too much is a bad habit because sometimes these folks don't seem to know how to conclude a thought and you'll notice that they end every sentence with *because, and,* or *but* so their words become a landslide of verbiage, but they also have a problem with summarizing because they feel like they've got to tell every minute detail and because of this self perpetuating style of one-sided conversation, it can be very difficult to jump in and bring it to a satisfying conclusion, but for the sake of your group, you, as leader, must find a way and a good way to do that is to follow the following suggestions and…

➢ Take notes as the person talks. This will tend to slow them down and give you a reason to interrupt them.
➢ Listen for repetition. Since they don't know how to quit when they've finished saying what they had to say, they'll start saying again what they've already said.
➢ Interrupt them politely the instant you hear them repeat something. Ask if what you've written in your notes describes their prayer request correctly.

STUDY GUIDE:

1. Some people think prayer requests should be presented to _____, not _____ _____.

2. In some groups, _____ is the unstated, but primary purpose of the group.

3. The power of your group's prayer has very much to do with their _____ and practically nothing to do with how _____ _____ they are.

Discussion question: List the groups in which you participate in group prayer. Beside each one, indicate whether the prayer requests are more like prayer, sharing, or gossip? Then rate the importance of sharing prayer requests for each group on a scale of 1 to 5.

Part Four

Guiding Group Prayer

Jehoshaphat bowed with his face to the ground, and all the people of Judah and Jerusalem fell down in worship before the LORD. Then some Levites from the Kohathites and Korahites stood up and praised the LORD, the God of Israel, with very loud voice.

2 Chronicles 20:18-19 (NIV)

Chapter 16

Guiding a Prayer Walk

Topical Prayer in Motion

The only agenda you need is praying for the needs that you see.

Who knows when and where prayer walking got started, but it seems to date to the 1970's when walking and jogging for exercise were really taking hold. It was a very natural thing, as Christians jogged through their neighborhoods, to start praying for the needs that they saw.

Prayer walking today is used in hundreds of different situations, but the essence of it is still the same - getting out where the needs are and praying for them as you see them.

Prayer Walking with a regular Partner

If you have a walking or jogging partner who's willing, try prayer walking. Just pray for needs that you see or those that come to mind as you walk or run. Keep in mind that prayer walking isn't for show. The people that see you go by every day need not realize you're praying for them.

In fact, you may remember that Jesus said that the prayers of the Pharisees, who made a big show of praying conspicuously on the street corners, had no effect. (Matthew 6:5) You sure don't want to be like them. Prayer walking's a

God thing. The only agenda you need is praying for the needs that you see.

However, once you start praying this way, you'll begin to see the area in a whole new light and become aware of opportunities for sharing the love of Jesus that you never saw before. You'll not be able to do more than pray for most of these needs, but don't limit the Lord. If He reveals an opportunity for witness or ministry and the Holy Spirit gives you a nudge, don't be afraid to follow His lead.

I know a missionary couple who've been starting house churches for many years. Prayer walking as a couple has become one of the cornerstones of their ministry. They say,

"Prayer walking is our passion...it helps set the pace and the direction for much of our work. It helps us as we cast our vision. We basically take an integrated approach to our prayer walks:

➤ We 'map' areas where we walk, observing what's going on in that area of town, and silently praying as we go, claiming this area for the Lord, and asking Him how this area can best be reached for Christ."

➢ We discuss topics of concern, burdens, problems, personal joys and sorrows, as we walk.

➢ We talk to persons with whom we have come in contact on some of our routes, forming casual relationships which can be deepened as we continue to come in contact with them.

➢ We also share tracts as we walk, as the Spirit leads." [4]

OK, maybe you're not a missionary starting house churches and sharing tracks isn't appropriate where you live, but don't limit what God can or can't do. Just walk and pray and let the Lord guide your steps, and your eyes, and your prayers. It might be helpful to think of prayer walking as topical prayer in motion.

Group Prayer Walking

(If you're in charge of the prayer time before or after the walk; go to chapters 18 or 20 for help with guiding prayer meetings.)

If you're asked to lead a large group, like a prayer walk around the school by parents the night before See You at the Pole, it's more like a lot of people doing individual prayer walks. Instruct them on the basics of prayer walking from the previous section on prayer walking with a partner and have them pray silently for the needs that come to mind as they walk.

In situations like this, leaders will sometimes provide a printed prayer sheet for folks to follow as they walk. It may include scriptures to meditate on, lists of needs, or even a suggested prayer. This is helpful especially if the group has many who are new to this form of prayer. The prayer sheet for the very first See You at the Pole prayer walk had these suggestions:

---

[4] Rob and Phyllis Hefner are missionaries for the International Mission Board of the Southern Baptist Convention serving in Brazil.

1. Pray for unbelievers to be saved and believers to grow spiritually.
2. Pray for spirit-filled students grounded in God's Word.
3. Pray for student self-worth and strength to handle peer pressure.
4. Pray for student potential and leadership.,
5. Pray for forgiveness and parental role models.
6. Pray for purity and healthy relationships.
7. Pray for alertness to satanic influences.

You can see how this would be helpful to those who aren't familiar with prayer walking. If you want to do something like this, you'll find the chapters on prayer meetings helpful. However, an extensive printed prayer guide misses the point for most prayer walking, which is to get into the situation and pray for the needs as you see them.

After the prayer walk, the group or groups will usually get together to report and give testimonies of what God has revealed. If you're leading this prayer time, chapters 18 and 20 will be helpful.

Prayer walks are best with groups of two or three. Situations where you might be asked to lead a group like this include preparation for a church evangelistic event, preparation for an outreach strategy while on a mission trip, or some similar situation.

These are generally one-time events in which you are likely to be leading folks who've never done a prayer walk before. Here are a couple of issues to consider.

Praying Silently or Out Loud?

It's a general principle of prayer, that praying out loud is better. Whether you're prayer walking alone or with a group, if the situation allows, try praying out loud. However, don't be like the Pharisees, praying out loud for the attention of men.

The missionary couple I mentioned prays silently because their situation involves crowded sidewalks in a very large city. As they walk, they talk with each other about what they are seeing. When they observe something they want to pray about, they both pray silently as they continue to walk.

That format will work in almost any situation and group. However, a suburban neighborhood with big yards and few people on the street would allow the group to try it both ways.

Should the group stop to pray?

Whether or not to stop and pray for a particular place or situation is a judgment call based on the situation, instructions given you by church leadership, and the guidance of the Holy Spirit.

You'll be tempted to think that if the group stops on the sidewalk and has a brief prayer meeting it will be a great witness to those who see you. In some situations, that's true, but more often it feeds right into the self-righteous stereotype the world has about Christians.

If you're starting a mission, preaching point, or backyard Bible club, and the group gathers around to dedicate that spot to the Lord, great. But if you stop on someone else's turf and huddle up for prayer right in front of them, that's not so good.

Try to see it from the world's point of view. What's the first thing you're going to do? What we naturally do when we pray as a group, face each other and bow. What have you just done? Turned your backs on the very ones you're concerned about.

You've provided just the image Satan wants to seer into the mind of every lost man, self-righteous Christians with their backs turned to him.

The power of prayer walking is not bringing your prayers to the streets, but bringing the power of the Holy Spirit to the streets through your prayer.

There's been plenty written about prayer walking. Some liken it to God's CIA, sending covert operatives into the enemy's camp. Others describe it as spiritual warfare with prayer warriors carrying the battle to the front lines of demonic conflict.

That may or may not be true in your situation, but deciphering the philosophy of prayer walking is not our concern. Leading a group to do it is, so let's follow our familiar prayer progression to plan a one time prayer walk involving two or three people.

Preparation:

Before the Prayer Walk

➢ Read the preceding section on prayer walking with a partner.
➢ Read the Old Testament book of Joshua in your daily devotions, particularly chapters 5 and 6.
➢ Review chapters 11 & 12 on prayer by suggestion and topical prayer.
➢ Drive or even walk through the area you've been assigned. Take some notes about what you see and feel.
➢ Decide what you think the route should be. Prepare a map if necessary.
➢ Make arrangements for transportation if needed.
➢ Find a small notepad you can carry with you on the prayer walk.

Just before the Prayer Walk

➢ Meet with your group at a central location, like the church, for a time of instruction and prayer. This is often led by a church leader.

➤ Include a time of confession and repentance in preparation for the prayer walk to follow.

➤ Explain the four rules of topical prayer.

  o If your group wants to pray silently, you won't need topical prayer. As the group walks, someone will point out a need and then everyone will pray silently with their eyes open as they continue to walk.

As the Prayer Walk begins

➤ When you arrive at the location, be sure everyone understands:

  o The instructions given by the church leadership

  o The time period and planned route for the walk

  o What to do if they get separated (Exchange cell phone numbers.)

  o The rules of topical praying if you're going to pray out loud

➤ As the group starts out, use Biblical visualization to prepare the group. Jesus on the road to Emmaus, (Mark 16:12) would be an excellent scene to use.

Salutation:

➤ Begin the prayer with "Dear Father…" or the salutation of your choice. (chapter 5)

➤ Express your thankfulness and praise to Him in a conversational tone, just loud enough for the members of your group to hear. Be visual. In other words, thank and praise Him for things you see right then: the sky, clouds, people, shoes on your feet, etc.

Petition:

➤ Ask the Lord for protection.

➤ Ask the Lord to reveal needs and opportunities.

➤ Pray for the first need you see. Pray a one sentence prayer and stop without saying any benediction. You want the others to continue that prayer while the need is still in sight.

➤ Ask, "Will someone else pray for this now while we're still close by."

➤ Prompt the group as needed for the first few minutes and even remind them of the rules of topical prayer, but don't make it an issue. If they don't get it, don't worry about it.

➤ Include Jesus. One of the joyful things about a prayer walk is how the Lord becomes part of your group conversation. As you walk along you might say to your group, "Look at that big tree there in that beautiful yard. Wouldn't that be a perfect place for a back yard Bible club." Then, instead of responding directly to you, one of the other members may extend the conversation into prayer, "Lord, we're looking at that tree and thinking it would be great for a Bible club. Father, we just pray that one day children will be gathered there learning about you."

➤ Pray in a manner appropriate for the situation. Don't feel that the group has to be praying out loud all the time. You're likely to be in several different situations as you walk so lead them as seems appropriate for the circumstance.

➤ Stop and visit casually with people along the way, and don't hesitate to tell them what you're doing if they ask; but don't push and don't waste time.

Benediction:

➤ The prayer walk is basically one long conversation between God and the group, so when you come to the end, say a concluding prayer or ask one of the others to do so.
➤ The concluding prayer should have a benediction such as, "In Jesus' name, amen."

STUDY GUIDE:

1. The essence of prayer walking is getting out where the _____ are and praying for them as you _____ them.
2. Prayer walking is _____ _____ in motion.
3. Prayer walking works best with groups of _____ _____ _____.
4. When prayer walking, always pray out loud and never talk with strangers. True or False

Discussion question: What do you think the missionary couple means when they say that prayer walking helps them 'cast their vision'?

Chapter 17

Guiding a Short Prayer Time with a Small Group

Bible Study & Home Group Prayer

Make prayer a priority; don't let any lesser thing take its place.

For the purpose of this discussion, prayer *time*, as opposed to prayer *meeting*, refers to a time set aside for group prayer during a meeting that has some other primary purpose: most commonly at the beginning or end of a Bible study class. In many churches, these are the most consistent and effective prayer times, so make the most of them. This chapter will also apply to many small church mid-week services.

Making Prayer a Priority:

In a setting where time is limited, making prayer a priority is the first issue your group must settle. Have you ever conducted a profile of how your group uses its time? If not, try this;

➤ Ask a class member to come to class ten minutes early with a pen, notepad, and digital watch on which the seconds are easily seen.

➤ Have them start taking notes as people arrive. They are to make note of the beginning of every event.

➤ In the left margin, they are to note the exact time.

Such a profile might look like this:

09:55:03	Class members start to arrive.
10:00:00	Time for class to start, people still coming in, everybody visiting.
10:13:46	Class president calls class to order and asks for announcements or class business.
	etc., etc., etc.
10:22:05	President turns the class over to teacher.
10:22:08	Teacher asks for prayer requests.
	etc., etc., etc.
10:25:49	Teacher begins prayer. Several people pray.
10:27:32	Teacher concludes prayer.
10:27:45	Teacher asks everyone to open Bibles.

10:28:08	Teacher asks a class member to read the first scripture.
10:32:11	Teacher asks a discussion question and several offer their opinions.
10:36:26	Teacher asks another class member to read the next Bible verse.
10:37:03	Teacher gives background of verse.
10:42:49	Class member asks question and several offer opinions.
10:45:13	Teacher asks class member to read the next scripture.
10:45:35	Teacher explains the verse.
10:52:23	Teacher apologizes for not finishing the lesson and asks everyone to stand for the closing prayer.
10:52:30	Teacher asks a class member to lead the closing prayer.
10:52:51	End of prayer. Class dismissed.

From this profile we can determine how the class above is using its time:

➤ just over nineteen minutes visiting (including the early arrivals),

➤ eighteen minutes reading scripture and teaching,

➤ eight minutes with announcements and class business,

➤ six and a half minutes in discussion about the lesson,

➤ almost four minutes making prayer requests, and

➤ two minutes in prayer.

Prayer will typically account for the least amount of time. Most of us agree that prayer should be a priority, but other things just crowd it out.

Now, how can you make your small group an exception to the rule? How can you make prayer a priority? The solution's the same as it is for every other important thing in your life:

❑ Set your priorities.
❑ Create a plan based on your priorities.
❑ Educate everyone involved in the plan.
❑ Carry out the plan.
❑ Adjust the plan as needed.
❑ Re-educate as needed.
❑ Keep working the plan.

If you don't know how much of your group's time should be dedicated to prayer, start by doing a time profile of your class, then calculate how much time was spent doing the following:

_____	Fellowship
_____	Announcements and class business
_____	Prayer requests
_____	Prayer
_____	Teaching
_____	Discussion of Bible lesson by class members

Discuss the results with your group and make a realistic schedule that gives prayer its appropriate priority. Such a schedule might look like this:

Our Bible Study Class
Class time: 10:00 – 10:50

10:00	fellowship time
10:05	class business
10:10	prayer time
10:20	teaching the Word
10:50	dismiss

Once the schedule is agreed upon, post it in the room for all to see. Of course, that will do no good unless the leaders of the class are committed to it. For instance, when it's 10:10 and the class is still discussing business, the leader of the class should say, "Our time's up for business and we don't want to use up our prayer time, so we'll have to continue this discussion later."

That's how you make prayer a priority; schedule it and don't let any lesser thing take its place. Now that you've made prayer a priority, you need to prepare well for the time your group has dedicated to prayer.

Preparation:

If you haven't studied the section on preparation in chapter 5, please do so now. Most prayer leaders are not accustomed to preparing for prayer the way they do for devotionals and other public speaking responsibilities. Some even feel that group prayer should be completely spontaneous with no preparation at all.

Guiding prayer effectively requires preparation and usually some notes to use during the prayer time. If that makes you uncomfortable, take a look at the 980 word prayer King Solomon prayed when he dedicated the temple in 2 Chronicles 6.

The prayer is not only beautiful; it's prophetic because he prays for the nation in captivity. Think about that. He's praying at the very zenith of Israel's power and prosperity, yet he prays about a time in which the people would be slaves in a foreign country. That didn't happen until hundreds of years later. I'd say he'd spent some time with the Lord preparing for this prayer.

If you want to lead group prayer more effectively than what you've experienced in the past, preparation is a must and for most of us, that will include using some notes.

Solomon was a really smart guy and probably didn't use notes, but for me, any time I'm doing something complicated and/or important, I use notes. I bet you do too. Why? Because notes give you confidence even if you don't have to use them.

Having said all that, don't get in over your head by planning a prayer time you can't handle. If you've never used the techniques described in Part 3, don't try to use them all. Start with what you're most comfortable with.

Also, if your time is limited to four or five minutes, you won't be able to use all the techniques. The following suggestions include all of them and assume you have ample time. Pick and choose what's appropriate for your situation.

Before the meeting checklist:

☐ Talk to the Lord about your group's prayer life during your daily devotional time.

☐ Find a notepad and pen that you can handle easily with your Bible during the prayer time.

☐ Locate a scripture to use for meditation (chapter 13) and mark it in your Bible. This could be a verse from the passage the group will be studying.

☐ Write down a Biblical situation to use at the beginning of the prayer time for visualization.. (chapter 14) Practice painting this word picture by seeing it in your mind, then describing it out loud as vividly as you can.

☐ Write down needs you anticipate the group will bring up as prayer requests. In some situations it's helpful to provide this list to the group.

☐ Introduce topical prayer (chapter 12) to several people ahead of time if it will be new to this group.

When it's time to pray:

➤ Explain that you're going to lead the session a little differently. Explain briefly the principles of topical prayer.
➤ Have prayer requests as you feel led. Don't let this eat up the time. See chapter 15 for help.
➤ Ask them to bow their heads and think about the scripture you're going to read. Read the scripture you selected previously. If it's brief, read it two or three times.
➤ Ask them to see themselves in the Biblical situation you selected earlier. Describe it briefly but vividly.

Salutation:

➤ Begin the prayer with the salutation of your choice.(chapter 5)
➤ Give your personal praise and thanksgiving. Be brief.
➤ Guide the group in a time of silent praise and thanksgiving using prayer by suggestion (chapter 11). Make a suggestion, pray the prayer silently, and then make the next suggestion. It could go like this, "As you begin your conversation with the Heavenly Father, why don't you thank Him for your family… thank Him for what He's done for you today… praise Him for the beauty of this day… etc." After three or four of these suggestions they'll have the idea and you should be silent for ten or fifteen seconds as they continue their silent praise.

Petition:

➤ Have a time of repentance early in the prayer time. Continuing to use prayer by suggestion, remind them that sin is a

hindrance to prayer. Suggest that they talk to the Lord about any sin in their life. If you're already 'prayed-up' for the day, be careful you don't rush them. This will be the main issue for some of your group.
➤ Open the session to individual prayers when you feel that the group's ready. Say something like this, "As we continue in prayer, I would like for you to pray out loud, one at a time, as you feel led. As you pray, please pray briefly for one issue at a time. This will give others the opportunity to join their prayer with yours. We will continue to pray about that one request until someone introduces a different need. I'll begin."
➤ Make the suggestion that someone lead the group to a new topic if you hear a prayer that's repetitious of a previous prayer. Usually two or three prayers on one topic are enough. After that, the prayers will tend to repeat or folks will fall back into the old habit of long monologue prayers. When the group's first learning to pray topically, you may need to do this often.
➤ Glance at your list of requests when you feel that the prayer time is coming to a conclusion or time's running out. Use prayer by suggestion to guide the group to pray for the remaining requests.
➤ Let the group know that you're about to conclude the session by asking if anyone still has a burden that they need to pray about.

Benediction:

➤ Thank the Lord for His presence and attention to the requests that have been made.
➤ Conclude with the benediction of your choice. (chapter 5)

STUDY GUIDE:

1. To make prayer a priority; _____ it and don't let any _____ thing take its place.

2. When doing something complicated and/or important, it's good to use _____, because they give you _____.

3. After the group has begun praying out loud, it's OK to interrupt and give instructions when needed. True or False

Discussion question: Explain the difference in a prayer *time* and a prayer *meeting*.

PRAYER GUIDE by Lowell Snow

Chapter 18

Guiding an Extended Prayer Meeting with a Small Group

Prayer Ministry & Other Meetings Devoted Entirely to Prayer

Guide everyone into the presence of God and help them express their needs to Him.

Perhaps the greatest opportunity for a prayer-guide is to lead a small group prayer meeting. Before diving in, let's be sure we understand a couple of terms.

By small group we mean a group that's small enough for everyone to pray. Five to fifteen would be normal. The most familiar example is the prayer ministry group, but these prayer warriors usually have specific instructions as to how to conduct their prayer meetings so we'll not focus on them. However, if you lead such a group, applying the preparations and procedures detailed here will help raise these meetings to a new level of intimacy with God.

The other term is prayer 'meeting' as opposed to a shorter prayer 'time' associated with a meeting that has some other primary purpose. A prayer meeting is devoted exclusively to prayer. If you're leading a meeting that also includes Bible study and/or a significant time of worship, you'll find chapters 17 and 19 helpful.

One type of small group prayer meeting is the home prayer meeting called in preparation for an evangelistic crusade. Less common are informal groups that come together with a mutual concern for some specific need.

Whatever the situation, your goal is to guide everyone into the presence of God and help them express their needs to Him. This is no small task. You must make good use of whatever time you have to prepare for this responsibility.

Preparation:

Before the meeting checklist:

☐ Ask God to give you insight into His purpose for this meeting during your daily devotional time.

☐ Find a notepad and pen that you'll be able to handle easily with your Bible during the meeting.

☐ Take notes as God gives you insight about the upcoming prayer meeting.

☐ Write down general things you feel the whole group should pray for at the beginning of the meeting. Examples are; God's protection of the place where you're meeting, freedom for the Holy Spirit to guide the meeting, greater faith, etc.

☐ Write down the names of two songs if singing's possible. They need to be so familiar that they can be sung without music or words. If you can't lead them yourself, arrange to have someone who can.

☐ Locate a scripture to use for scriptural meditation at the beginning of the prayer time and mark it in your Bible. The concordance in the back of your Bible will give you ideas. (chapter 13)

☐ Write down a Biblical situation that you can use for visualization at the beginning of the prayer time. Practice painting this word picture by seeing it in your mind, then describing it out loud as vividly as you can. (chapter 14)

☐ Decide how you're going to do prayer requests and make necessary preparations. (chapter 15)

☐ Educate several people ahead of time in the rules of topical prayer if it will be new to this group. (chapter 12)

At the meeting:

☐ Arrive at the location of the prayer meeting early. Determine where and how the group will sit during the prayer time.

☐ Arrange seating in a circle if possible. If you'll need to move furniture, talk to the host about what you have in mind.

☐ Check for ventilation. A small room, filled with people, can get pretty stuffy. If there's central air conditioning, ask the host to set it so that the fan runs continually.

☐ Locate your spot and reserve it. You need to be where everyone can hear and see you.

☐ Announce a start time for the prayer meeting so that refreshments and fellowship won't infringe on the real purpose of the gathering.

☐ Look over your notes.

☐ Ask everyone to start congregating in the prayer area ten minutes before the prayer time. As they do, direct them to sit in the way you've determined will work best. Ask them to move furniture or bring chairs from other parts of the house as discussed with the host above.

As the meeting begins:

➢ Start the meeting on time.
➢ Thank everyone for coming. Thank the host if you're in a home.
➢ Be sure everyone realizes the purpose for which this prayer meeting was called.
➢ Explain briefly the principles of topical prayer.
➢ Have prayer requests as you feel led. (chapter 15)
➢ Sing a song or two. Skip this if there's not a good leader available.
➢ Ask them to bow their heads and think about the scripture you're going to read. Read the scripture you selected previously. If it's brief, read it two or three times.

➢ Ask them to see themselves in the Biblical situation you selected earlier. Describe it briefly but vividly.

Salutation:

➢ Begin the prayer with the salutation of your choice.(chapter 5)

➢ Give your personal praise and thanksgiving to Him. Keep this very brief; this prayer time is not about you.

➢ Suggest that the group give praise and thanksgiving to God silently. Make a suggestion, pray the prayer yourself silently, then make the next suggestion.

Petition:

➢ Lead a time of repentance using prayer by suggestion.
  ✓ Remind them that sin is a hindrance to prayer. Suggest that they talk to the Lord about any sin in their life, repent, and ask for forgiveness.
  ✓ Wait several seconds, then remind them that God already knows about their sin; He's just waiting for them to get honest and humble.
  ✓ Don't rush this part. If the prayer meeting is to be effective with God, the group has to get their hearts right.

➢ Guide the group to pray in agreement, using prayer by suggestion, about the issues you wrote down during your preparation. These should conclude with issues that get to the purpose of the meeting.

➢ Open the session to topical prayer. Say something like this, "Jesus told us that there's amazing power when we agree with Him and with each other in prayer. As we continue in prayer, I would like you to pray out loud, one at a time, for one issue at a time. Pray loud enough for everyone to hear so we can pray along with you silently. I will begin."

➢ Don't say a benediction after you pray, just stop. Wait a few seconds so the group will understand that you have prayed one simple prayer for one issue, then say, "Now, would two or three of you continue this prayer?"

➢ Let the prayer session have a life of it's own as it's led by the Holy Spirit. However, there may be times that you need to step in with further instruction or insight. For instance, the group may begin praying about an issue that you realize they need more information about. Say something like this, "I want to interrupt the prayer time for a moment. Please open your eyes and look this way. I believe we need a little more information about this issue before we continue." It may be that you know about the issue or you may want to ask someone else to give the group further insight. When that's done, ask the group to continue the prayer.

➢ Glance at your notes to see if there's anything that still needs to be covered in prayer. Use prayer by suggestion to cover these remaining needs.

➢ Ask if anyone still has a burden that they need to pray about. If no one prays, say, "I feel that it's time to conclude our prayer so let me offer our benediction." If you feel led, ask someone in the group to say the benediction.

Benediction:

➢ Thank the Lord for His presence and attention to the requests that have been made.

➢ Ask for His blessings on the hosts and anyone else who has made sacrifices to make the prayer meeting possible.

➢ Conclude with the benediction of your choice. (chapter 5)

After the Meeting:

➤ Be considerate guests. When the prayer session's over, there are three issues you need to take care of: thanks, furniture, and trash. Don't try to do all this yourself. People want to be helpful, but they may need you to get them organized.
- Encourage the group to express appreciation to the hosts.
- See that any rearranged furniture is returned to its original positions. It's a good idea to do this even if you're meeting in a church building.

- See that the area is cleaned up and trash disposed of. (If you're meeting in a church building, be certain that someone's responsible for turning off lights and locking up.)

➤ Deal with the after-glow. If, while most folks are leaving, some seem 'entrenched', give these stragglers a friendly hint not to stay too long. Your hosts will appreciate it.
➤ Write a thank you note to the hosts when you get home, and to any others who were helpful.

STUDY GUIDE:

1. A *small group* will include not less than four and not more than eight people. True or False

2. Your goal is to guide everyone into the _____ ____ _____ and help them express their _____ to Him.

3. If the prayer meeting is to be effective with God, the group has to _____ _____ _____ _____ with Him.

4. When the prayer session's over, there are three issues you need to take care of: _____, _____, and _____.

Discussion question: Can you think of some situations that would warrant the calling of a small group prayer meeting?

Chapter 19

Guiding a Short Prayer Time with a Large Group

Mid-week Service – Groups Over 15 in Attendance

Whether it's the faithful twenty-five meeting in the fellowship hall on Wednesday night or 25,000 in a huge venue, your goal's the same; guide them into the presence of God to talk with Him about their needs.

In most situations, you'll want to use large group techniques for a group over fifteen. Let's remind ourselves of the definition of a prayer time.

A prayer time (as opposed to a prayer meeting) is a time set aside for group prayer during a meeting that has a primary purpose other than prayer. Generally, you'll have a time limit of less than fifteen minutes and people in attendance who do not usually participate in public prayer.

The largest prayer time I've ever witnessed was a denominational meeting in a convention center and involved over 20,000 people. More typical would be the prayer time during a mid-week worship service. Other large group prayer times you might find yourself leading would be large Bible Study classes, retreats, and conferences.

Whether it's the faithful twenty-five meeting in the fellowship hall on Wednesday night or 25,000 in a huge venue, your goal's the same; guide them into the presence of God to talk with Him about their needs.

Just as the purpose remains the same, some of the techniques we've already learned will carry over. Prayer by suggestion, scripture meditation, and Biblical visualization, scale up to any size group with little or no change in method. See chapters 11, 13, & 14.

On the other hand, topical praying (chapter 12) will require some modification. Here are some topical prayer techniques that you may find useful in large group prayer times. With all these methods, be sure to give those who are afraid to pray out loud some way to participate.

➤ **Huddle groups -** The prayer leader that guided those 20,000 convention-goers asked everyone to huddle up in groups of three to five, then asked them to pray, round-robin style, for some particular needs that he suggested. This works great in groups where you know that the majority don't mind praying out loud. Even so, make it clear that they can participate without praying publicly.

✓ Another, more time consuming, but personal version of this is to pass out note cards to everyone. Ask them to write down a prayer request and give it to another person in their huddle group. Then give the groups time to pray, round-robin style, for each other.

➤ **Topical prayer groups** – Divide the group into small groups with leaders prepared to lead topical prayer.

➤ **Divided requests** - If you have a printed prayer list, divide it up then separate the group into corresponding sections.

✓ Another version of this is to read a request, then assign it to a particular section of the congregation or group. You might have the folks sitting in that section repeat the name out loud to help them remember it.

➤ **Volunteer topical prayer leaders** - If the situation is such that a person standing in the group can be heard by everyone, and the group's accustomed to topical prayer, ask people to voluntarily stand, one at a time, and pray topically.

➤ **Appointed topical prayer leaders** - Call on a few individuals to pray out loud on a topic that you give them.

➤ **Personal needs** – Ask people to stand or come to the altar who want to be prayed for. Then ask others to come around them and pray for them. Depending on the situation, you can call on someone to pray out loud or just let those gathered around them pray for them.

✓ Another version of this is to make prayer request cards available to the whole group. These are collected then dispersed in some fashion for immediate prayer. They can be dispersed back to the group or placed at the altar for volunteers to come and pray for.

✓ In large congregations, they may be turned over to a prayer ministry or to the deacons who pray for each one as the worship service continues. In some services, after praying over them, the deacons bring these cards back to a special place in the altar area.

➤ **Common needs** – Name a particular need and ask those with that need to stand or come to the altar. This could be folks who've lost jobs, are separated from their children, have cancer, or some other specific situation. Just do one at a time so there's no confusion. Then ask those whom God has helped through a similar problem to go and pray for them.

There are a thousand ways to involve God's people in topical prayer. Once you get in the flow, you'll be surprised how the Holy Spirit will guide you.

It's important to stay within the *acceptance* zone of your group. It's not helpful to make prayer a controversy. You don't have to stay in their *comfort* zone all the time, but be careful. There's a mathematical formula in the church that looks like this:

Change = Conflict

The greater the change, the greater the conflict, so make changes gradually.

Now, let's assume you have the opportunity to lead a Bible study group of fifty in a ten to fifteen minute prayer time. We'll imagine that they're accustomed to having a prayer time, but in the past have only had monologue prayers. They want a more intimate encounter with the Lord and just need a little guidance.

The following outline focuses on using the four techniques discussed in chapters 11 - 14. Most of the time is given to prayer by suggestion because this is the easiest and most effective way to guide everyone into an encounter with God. A brief time of volunteer topical praying concludes the prayer time.

Preparation:

Before the meeting checklist:

☐ Pray for God's blessing and direction during your daily devotional time.

☐ Have your notepad and pen close at hand.

☐ Locate a scripture to use for meditation (chapter 13) and mark it in your Bible.

☐ Write down and practice a Biblical situation to use If there will be time for visualization. (chapter 14)

☐ Make arrangements for copies of the group's prayer list to be printed and distributed. (chapter 15)

☐ Prepare an outline of the prayer time. Include any notes you'll need like the rules of topical prayer, etc.

When its time to pray:

If you aren't the person that normally leads the group in prayer, a leader of the group should introduce you and explain that you've been asked to lead the prayer time. This is important because you'll be leading them differently than they're used to. They'll be more inclined to follow your lead if you've been introduced.

For instructional purposes, the rest of this chapter includes a sample prayer in the right column that follows along with the instructions in the left column.

Instructions	Sample Prayer
➤ Don't waste time. Get straight to the matter of prayer.	"I will be your prayer guide for the next few minutes. Instead of me saying the prayer or asking some of you to lead, I'm going to guide each of you into the presence of God and encourage you to encounter Him personally.

➢ Have prayer requests only if needed. Take notes if anyone makes an addition to the list. (chapter 15)

➢ Explain briefly the four rules of topical prayer.

➢ Ask them to bow their heads and use your scripture meditation to focus their attention on the things of God. The words in **bold** would be emphasized as you read.

The prayer list was available as you came in. Is there anyone who didn't get one? - We want to maximize our time with the Lord, praying for these needs, so we'll not discuss the list unless there's something that needs to be added.

When it comes time to pray out loud, I'll ask that we all 'agree' in prayer by praying about one thing at a time. This is called topical praying. There are four simple rules:

1. Each person prays a short prayer about one topic at a time.
2. Each person can pray as often as they want.
3. The group continues praying about the same topic until someone introduces another topic.
4. Each topical prayer is part of the whole and doesn't need a benediction.

By praying for one issue at a time, it will be easier for all of us to stay focused on that one need and therefore, agree, as we bring that petition to our Heavenly Father. Now let me repeat those four rules of topical prayer. (repeat the four rules)

Now, would you bow your heads and listen to the words of this scripture.

Again, I tell you that if two of you on earth **agree** about anything **you** ask for, it will be done for **you** by my Father in heaven. For where two or three come **together** in my name, there am I with **them**.
(Matthew 18:19-20 NIV)

Again, I tell you that if two of you on earth **agree** about **anything** you ask for, it will be **done** for you by my **Father** in heaven. For where **two or three** come together **in my name**, there am I with them.

➤ Guide them into the presence of God using Biblical visualization.

Again, I tell you that if two of you on earth **agree** about anything you **ask** for, it **will** be done for you by my Father in heaven. **For** where two or three come together **in my name**, **there** am I **with** them.

Before you begin your conversation with God, I would like for you to imagine that you're in the Heavenly throne room. The Bible says it's so big that a hundred million angels can gather there to praise the Lord. As you step through the entry, it's so immense that looking across the floor toward the throne is like looking out across an ocean.

As we all walk across this great expanse we get closer and closer to the throne. In front of the throne you come to a great golden altar with the smoke of sweet incense rising above it. This is the altar of prayer and the smoke represents the prayers of God's people from all around the world going up before Him continually.

The throne room of heaven is a real place. It's the place you go spiritually every time you pray. Can you see yourself there, now? The Creator of the universe has granted you an audience. What are you going to do? What are you going to say?

Salutation:

➤ Say a brief monologue prayer of salutation to the Lord.

Dear Heavenly Father,

It never ceases to amaze us that you welcome us into your presence. You're so holy and righteous and powerful. We love you and love your creation. Please protect us, bless us, and even guide us as we talk to you today.

➢ Guide the group to give personal praise and thanksgiving to God silently using prayer by suggestion. (Remember to pace your suggestions by praying silently for the same thing you've suggested to them.)

This symbol represents times of silent prayer between suggestions.

Right now, would you praise Him silently? Begin by praising Him for something beautiful in His creation.

Now praise Him for something wonderful He's done. Perhaps something from scripture or something He's done for you or someone you know.

Now, would you give thanks to Him for the blessings in your life? Be specific. The Bible says that all good things are from the Father.

Petition:

➢ Continue prayer by suggestion to bring them into a time of confession. Don't rush. Allow enough time to do each thing you suggest.

As you continue in silent prayer, would you ask God to reveal anything in your life that's not pleasing to Him? Nothing's hidden from Him. Be humble and honest. He doesn't accept excuses or passing the blame to someone else. Confess your sin to Him. Put a name on it.

Now, ask your Heavenly Father what He wants you to do about your sin. Is there some restitution or apology that needs to be made to another person? Perhaps He just wants you to except His forgiveness and put it behind you.

Thank Him for His forgiveness and promise Him that you'll do anything He's asked you to do.

➢ Guide them to pray for kingdom needs.

Jesus taught us to pray for His kingdom work around the world. Do you know any missionaries or ministers personally? Pray for the specific needs of their families and ministries. If you don't know their needs, ask the Holy Spirit to guide your prayer.

➢ Guide them into a time of supplication for the needs of others. If you've had prayer requests, use them here.

Now, would you pray in the same way for the persons seated next to you? Pray for them as specifically as you can.

There are many needs on our prayer list. Would you pray specifically for those that the Lord has given you a burden for.

➢ Guide them to pray for their own needs.

Is there a struggle in your life that you need to bring before God today? He loves you more than you can imagine and wants to help you right now. Are you fighting with some temptation? Is there a physical or emotional burden? Perhaps a relationship that's gone wrong or a decision you have to make? Tell your Heavenly Father about it.

In your spirit, wrap that problem up in a bundle of faith and lay it on the floor before the throne of God.

Now ask Him to guide you in dealing with this issue.

➢ When you feel that the group's ready, open the session to topical prayers.

For the next few minutes, we'll pray out loud, one at a time, for one issue at a time. Remember; Jesus taught us to agree together in prayer. As someone prays out loud for something the Lord has placed on their heart, you pray silently for that same need. Keep in mind those four rules for topical prayer:

1. Each person prays a short prayer about one topic at a time.
2. Each person can pray as often as they want.
3. The group continues praying about the same topic until someone introduces another topic.
4. Each topical prayer is part of the whole and doesn't need a benediction.

I'd like to pray first. Dear Father, I want to lift up my friend _____, who's having a real struggle. Please help him right now to know that we love him.

Now, would two or three of you continue this prayer for our friend _____?

➤ Guide them to a new topic when you hear a prayer that's repetitious, usually the third or fourth prayer. Continue to prompt them in this way if necessary.

I'm sure there are many issues that we want to agree on in prayer and our time's limited. Would someone continue our prayer now about a different issue? It can be someone who has already prayed or someone who hasn't. It doesn't matter, but someone continue our prayer by leading us in prayer about a new topic.

➤ Bring the prayer time to a conclusion at the appropriate time. You want them to look forward to the next time.

Our time's running out, but we don't want to prevent someone from praying that has a need. If there's someone else that needs to pray, and hasn't had an opportunity, please do so now.

Benediction:

➤ Thank the Lord for His presence.

Dear Father, we are so thankful for the privilege to talk with you about these needs. We love you and praise you.

➤ Conclude with a benediction of your choice. (chapter 5)

It's in the name of Jesus that we pray, amen."

The more you lead a group this way, the less you'll need to intervene in the topical part of the prayer. It is, after all, the way we carry on our day to day conversations. With practice, it becomes very natural.

STUDY GUIDE:

1. A prayer time is usually less than _____ minutes.

2. Of the four techniques, _____ _____ is the only one that has to be modified for large groups.

3. When introducing new ways of praying, it's important to stay within people's _____ zone, but OK to nudge them out of their _____ zone.

Discussion question: This chapter contains a detailed sample prayer time using the prayer guide techniques. In the circumstance where you most often experience group prayer, do you feel that this way of leading prayer would be more or less beneficial to your group than the round-robin methods described in chapter 10? Why?

PRAYER GUIDE by Lowell Snow

Chapter 20

Guiding an Extended Prayer Meeting with a Large Group

Solemn Assembly – Congregational Call to Prayer

Many Christians have never experienced a large group prayer meeting,
which are rare even in Scripture.
Here are five examples:

<u>Prayer meeting</u>	<u>Result</u>
➢ Thousands of Jews gathered to pray in Jerusalem for deliverance from the Ammonites during the reign of King Jehoshaphat. 2 Chronicles 20	➢ God sent an angel to destroy the Ammonites.
➢ Esther called on all the Jews in Susa to gather for three days of fasting and prayer before she went to the King and asked for mercy. Esther 4:16	➢ The King received Esther, granted mercy to the Jews, and their enemies were destroyed.
➢ Israelites gathered in Jerusalem for worship, then repented in prayer for three hours after the Bible was read to them and they realized how sinful they were. Nehemiah 9:3	➢ The Jews signed a contract with God that could be considered the official beginning of modern Judaism.
➢ Over one hundred disciples prayed together for several days for the power to obey Christ's commission. Acts 1-2	➢ The Holy Spirit appeared as tongues of fire over each disciple and New Testament Christianity was born.
➢ A group of believers gathered at Mark's mother's house to pray for Peter in prison. Acts 12:12	➢ God sent an angel to the jail to wake Peter up and escort him out. When he showed up at the prayer meeting, they thought he was a ghost.

These examples of large group prayer meetings may seem random, but there are three similarities.

> The meeting is in response to a crisis.
> The prayers have a primary focus.
> The meetings are singular events.

You may be thinking that the early church had regular large group prayer meetings because of the following amazing description of those first Christians:

They **devoted themselves** to the apostles' teaching and to the fellowship, to the breaking of bread and to **prayer**. Everyone was filled with awe, and many wonders and miraculous signs were done by the apostles. All the believers were together and had everything in common. Selling their possessions and goods, they gave to anyone as he had need. **Every day they continued to meet together in the temple courts**. They broke bread in their homes and ate together with glad and sincere hearts, praising God and enjoying the favor of all the people. And the Lord added to their number daily those who were being saved.
Acts 2:42-47 (NIV)

Reading this, one can get the idea that they met every day in the temple court yard for a massive prayer meeting. However, if you look closely, it doesn't say that. They certainly met there daily and we can be certain that they prayed; however we can be equally sure that they taught the Bible and had worship. Therefore, for our purposes, it doesn't qualify as a prayer meeting because prayer was only part of the meeting.

There's no doubt that the Jerusalem church was a praying church, but there's no clear example of regular large group prayer meetings. My point is simply this; large group prayer meetings are most often called as a singular response to a crisis rather than being a scheduled part of church life.

Many churches have a regularly scheduled congregational prayer meeting, but it's usually a worship service in which an extended prayer time takes the place of the sermon. This is a great thing, but not what we're talking about in this chapter.

If your church never has services that are completely dedicated to prayer, you need to open your heart to this most powerful form of prayer. Hopefully, this chapter will give you the tools you need to conduct a large group prayer meeting whenever the church is facing a crisis or God-sized decision.

Before we go any farther, let me emphasize that this kind of prayer meeting should not be led by a novice. There are too many pitfalls. For one, the meeting is often called because of a crisis in which people's emotions are high. A prayer guide that's not full of the Holy Spirit and experienced in leading large groups can be manipulated by the evil one to cause great harm in the fellowship.

If you're to lead this kind of prayer meeting, you'll need the spiritual gifts of wisdom and discernment (I Corinthians 12:7-11) and exemplify the fruit of the Spirit as revealed in the following passage:

But the fruit of the Spirit is love, joy, peace, patience, kindness, goodness, faithfulness, gentleness and self-control. Against such things there is no law.
Galatians 5:22-23 (NIV)

If you do not possess these characteristics or if you're too close to the crisis to control your own emotions, you should decline from leading such a meeting.

This kind of meeting is also difficult because leading a large group of people to do something complicated that none of them has ever done before, is a real challenge.

Give yourself plenty of lead time and prepare well. Recruit the best people you can to help you and go through the whole service with them ahead of time. This will help you see potential problems.

For instance, the huddle group time in the plan that follows may seem fairly straight forward as you prepare, but when you go through it with a group; you may find that they don't understand your instructions at all. You might need to rewrite your instructions or perhaps print them on the back of every card.

This kind of prayer meeting is a challenge, but the potential rewards are heavenly. The following check lists and outlines will take you from preparation to benediction in leading a large group prayer meeting that could last an hour to an hour and a half. It involves most of the techniques and issues discussed to this point.

Preparation:

Preparation checklist:

☐ Do whatever it takes to get holy before God. Consider a personal fast. Consider suggesting that the group fast in preparation for the meeting.

☐ Pray for insight into the Lord's purpose for the meeting.

☐ Study the five Biblical examples of large group prayer meetings at the beginning of this chapter and read through the rest of this chapter.

☐ Re-read chapters 11 – 14 about the four group prayer techniques.

☐ Define the purpose of the meeting.
  o Put in writing what the group needs God to do for them.
  o Rewrite these needs as a prayer for the group to say together at the beginning of the meeting. Keep rewriting until you're satisfied that it expresses the true purpose of the meeting.

  o Leave off the benediction because the prayer will continue.
  o Ask someone to read it and give you feed back.
  o Type or print your best version with breaks every few words so you can guide the group to repeat the prayer a phrase at a time. Don't make copies for the group.

☐ Ask God to reveal the things He requires of the group before He can answer their prayers. For instance, He may be saying that He can't bless their prayers as long as they're unforgiving toward one another. Pray over these for as long as it takes to be sure you know the mind of God.

☐ Plan the service so that announcements, etc. are done at the beginning.

☐ Write out an outline of the service as you expect to lead it from beginning to conclusion. During the service, you'll be flexible and sensitive to the Holy Spirit, but you need to start with a plan.

☐ Consider who you might ask to say the closing prayer. This would need to be someone full of the Spirit and powerful in prayer. Contact that person and explain what you need them to do.

☐ Arrange for the building to be open, lighted, and air conditioned/heated. Be sure units are turned on several hours before the meeting.

☐ Communicate with the worship leader about music. Ask them to contact any musicians needed. Provide written instructions that express exactly what you want done and how much time there will be for music.
  o Note: when using instrumental music as a background it must not be distracting, so ask the musicians to use unfamiliar melodies. Some are adept at playing beautiful chords with no melody at all.

☐ Arrange for counselors for the altar calls. Don't count yourself as one. Schedule a meeting with them for prayer and instruction just before the service.

☐ Arrange to have note cards and pencils for the whole group. (see huddle group prayer time below) Make preparations for any other printed material the group will need.

☐ Arrange for ushers/greeters. Send detailed instructions to each of them and meet with them briefly before the meeting.

☐ Choose scriptures to use for meditations appropriate for the service you've planned.

☐ Select Biblical situations to use for the visualizations you've planned.

☐ Select a Biblical benediction (to use with the closing prayer) and write it in your notes or mark it in your Bible. (chapter 5)

☐ Determine what you'll use for the container in which to place the note cards when people bring them to the altar. It needs to be several inches deep so the cards can't be seen after they're dropped in and large enough to hold the cards from the entire group. A large brass pot would be a good choice.

☐ Have a training session for those who'll be helping with topical prayer sessions.

☐ Spend some time in the location where the prayer meeting will take place. Determine where and how you want the group to sit. If you expect the group to be kneeling for any part of the meeting, figure out how best to accomplish this for the number you expect. Keep in mind that many people can't get on their knees at all and most can't stay on their knees very long without a padded kneeling rail.

☐ Give prayerful consideration to how you expect factions within the group to sit. For instance, do you expect that students will tend to congregate in one area? Will those with differing opinions segregate? If you feel this will be detrimental to the meeting, have a plan for dealing with it. The best thing to do is ask them to sit in groups that de-emphasize the factions. (Be careful, you don't want to short circuit the meeting before the Holy Spirit has opportunity to work on their hearts.) Here are some possibilities:

o Sit as families.
o Sit as Bible study groups.
o If the church has a deacon ministry, have the families gather around their assigned deacons.
o Use something arbitrary like the month they were born in.

☐ Consider having a prayer walk around and through the facility before the meeting.

Before the meeting checklist:

☐ Be there early.
o Check lighting and air conditioning/heating.
o Check all preparations and make adjustments as needed.
o Meet with and give final instructions to the ushers.
o Pray with counselors and appropriate leaders.

As the meeting begins:

➤ Start on time. Don't wait for stragglers.
➤ Make necessary announcements.
➤ Explain the purpose for the meeting.
➤ Tell them that they'll be praying in small groups for part of the meeting and explain how you want them to divide. Have them stand, greet one another, and move so that they are arranged as you have suggested.
➤ Present the principles of topical prayer.
➤ Don't have prayer requests. Stick to the purpose for which the meeting was called.

➤ Have the group sing a song or two. Skip this if there's not a good leader available.
➤ Have the keyboardist continue with soft background music all the way through the first altar call.
➤ Begin with scripture meditation.
➤ Continue with a Biblical visualization.

Salutation:

➤ Begin the prayer with the salutation of your choice.(chapter 5)
➤ Give your personal praise and thanksgiving to Him.
➤ Use prayer by suggestion to guide the group in personal praise and thanksgiving.

Petition:

➤ Ask the Lord to protect the group during the meeting.
➤ Use the prayer you wrote during your preparation that expresses what the congregation needs God to do. Read it, one phrase at a time, asking the congregation to repeat it.
➤ Use Scripture meditation to begin a time of soul searching. Your time alone with God will have given you insight into the scriptures to use and what suggestions to make.
➤ Using prayer by suggestion, guide the group into a time of confession and repentance.
➤ Have an altar call at this point in the service. Of course you'll do it in a way that's appropriate for your congregation.
➤ Instruct the musicians to continue the background music until the altar call is concluded.
➤ Ask for three or four testimonies after the altar call is over and people have returned to their seats. Ask them to speak briefly about how God has been moving in their spirit. Remind them that you're not asking them to preach or give their opinions, but to share what God is doing. Be sensitive to the Spirit, but this shouldn't go more than five or, at most, ten minutes.

Small group prayer time:

➤ Remind them of the purpose for this prayer meeting.
➤ Tell them that for the next portion of the meeting you'll ask them to pray within their small groups, using the principles of topical praying.
➤ Move some people around if you need to so that each group has no more than fifteen people. If the groups need to rearrange chairs or move to different parts of the room, have them do so.
➤ Have the groups select a prayer leader at this time unless they're already assigned.
➤ Don't join a prayer group. You need to stay in a position where you can monitor all the groups.
➤ Explain again the principles of topical praying.
➤ Guide them back before the Lord using scripture meditation and perhaps a Biblical visualization.
➤ Open the session to individual prayers. Say something like this, "As we continue in prayer, I would like you to pray out loud, one at a time within your groups. As you pray, please pray briefly for one issue at a time. This will give others the opportunity to join their prayer with yours. For instance, if someone prays for the pastor, two or three others should also pray for the pastor. Then, someone else may want to pray for the finance committee and a few others will pray for that. The group continues to pray about one need at a time. The leader in each group will begin the prayer time now."
➤ Have some very soft background music so the groups don't distract each other. The

fewer groups you have, the more important this is.

➤ Observe the groups as they begin praying. If you see that a group's having trouble getting started, go to them quietly and see if you can facilitate their prayer time. Then go back to your place and continue to observe.

➤ Ask all the groups to bring their prayer time to a conclusion when you feel that this part of the prayer meeting has gone long enough, or if one of the groups concludes their prayer and starts visiting.

Huddle group prayer time:

➤ Now ask them to further divide their groups into huddles of two or three. You should not join a group.

➤ Have the ushers see that everyone has a pencil and note card as they begin getting into their huddle groups.

➤ Ask them to write down the first names of those in their huddle.

➤ Give them these instructions, walking them through the process one step at a time:

• The purpose of the huddle is to pray about the issue at hand as it relates to each person in the huddle.

• If an individual does not want to pray out loud they can participate silently.

• Each person is to finish this sentence on their note card, "This issue has caused me to feel _____, and I need God to help me by _____." (This should be printed either on the cards, or on something large enough for all to read.)

• After they've done this, they are to share their answers with the huddle.

• After one person shares their prayer need, another member of the huddle is to pray for them.

• Each person in the huddle should share and be prayed for in this fashion.

• When everyone in the group has been prayed for, each person is to bring their card to the altar, put them in the container, find a seat as close to the front as possible, and pray silently.

➤ Have this last instruction on a screen or large white board reminding them what to do when their group is through.

Letting God Speak:

➤ Have them all come to the altar area. Suggest that they get in a comfortable position. Some can sit in the pulpit area, pulpit steps, on the floor, or front pews. Get them close together, but not crowded.

➤ Tell them that before you continue the meeting with a time of group prayer, you would like to hear what God has been saying to them. Remind them that they are not to preach, but to briefly and humbly share what God has said to them.

➤ Ask them to raise their hand if they have something to say. If you have a cordless handheld microphone, carry or pass it to each one who stands.

• Sometimes, I like to keep the microphone in my hand. This way I can keep it close to their mouth so they are heard by all. Also, they don't tend to talk as long and I can interrupt to comment or ask questions. It's more like an interview.

➤ Don't overdo this. Four or five will probably be enough. If they start repeating, you've had too many, but be sensitive to the Holy Spirit.

Focus the large group prayer:

➢ Tell them that the final part of the prayer meeting needs to be focused on the primary issue. State it as concisely as you can.
➢ Share with them that you want as many people as can to pray, but that their prayers should be:

- Brief
- Specific
- Bold

➢ Write those words on a screen or white board.
➢ Remind them that they need to be praying silently in agreement with whoever is praying out loud.
➢ Tell them who will conclude.
➢ Use visualization to guide them into the heavenly throne room. (see the sample prayer in chapter 19)
➢ Have the worship leader, if possible, to lead a familiar song of adoration. Ask the people to sing it directly to the Lord as if they're in the throne room.
➢ Say the first prayer yourself as an example of how you want them to pray.

Benediction:

➢ Be sensitive to the Spirit as to when to close the meeting. Knowing when can be difficult. One thing to remember is that the prayer meeting isn't an end in itself.

➢ Be prepared to deal with folks that need additional prayer and/or counseling after the service.
- Before the benediction, make an announcement like this, "After we close the service, those of you who want to continue praying are welcome to stay in the altar area. One of our counselors or ministers will come to you and pray with you if you desire."
- Don't ask the congregation to exit the room if they aren't praying. Postlude music will cover these conversations and prayers.
- Be sure your counselors and ministers are prepared for this time. They should go to anyone who remains praying after the benediction and simply ask them if they would like prayer.
➢ Ask the person you contacted to offer the benediction.
➢ Use the Biblical benediction you selected during your preparation.
➢ Dismiss the group, reminding them that the altar is still open for prayer and counseling.
➢ Arrange for music to play for ten or fifteen minutes after the service concludes. This music should not be soft and moody, but upbeat even though there may still be people in the altar. The music will cover their prayers and private conversations while letting the rest of the congregation feel comfortable to talk as they disperse.
- Leaders will often ask the congregation to leave meetings like this without speaking. This may actually be a mistake as conversations after the service are often very significant.

STUDY GUIDE:

1. The five examples at the beginning of the chapter have three similarities: The meeting is in response to a _____. The prayers have a primary _____. The meetings are _____ events.

2. These meetings should not be lead by a _____ prayer guide.

3. Before leading such a meeting, do whatever it takes to get:

   A. a good musician,   B. holy,   or C. a video projector.

Discussion question: Name several situations is which you feel a church should consider calling a congregational prayer meeting.

Part Five

Guiding Prayer in Worship

And when they had prayed, the place where they were assembled together was shaken; and they were all filled with the Holy Spirit, and they spoke the word of God with boldness.   Acts 4:31 (NKJV)

Chapter 21

All God's People Want to Pray

A Pilgrimage of Prayer

It wasn't a matter of making them pray or praying for them, it was all about letting them pray.

My pilgrimage of prayer began when my father was saved and delivered from alcohol addiction while I was still a baby. From then on, he loved God and believed in prayer. Our family prayed before every meal and had family devotions at bedtime.

Dad also believed in going to church - a lot. Worship services, prayer meetings, visitation, mission groups: it didn't matter. If the door was unlocked at the church, we were there. In this conservative Protestant church where I literally grew up, prayer was predictable.

➤ Laymen led prayers at certain points during worship services.
➤ All meetings began and concluded with a prayer.
➤ The pastor led a pastoral prayer during the Sunday morning and evening service in which he prayed for the big stuff like church members in the hospital and world problems. On occasion, he would pray for missionaries, which usually meant we were about to take up a special offering.
➤ On Wednesday evening there was a prayer meeting. The first half of this

service consisted of two hymns, a lengthy discussion of the sick whose names were printed on colored paper, and a brief time of prayer in which the pastor called on three or four laymen to pray out loud. The rest of the hour was devoted to a Bible study.

Until my high school years, I had no reason to think there was any other way to do prayer in the church. Then some Pentecostal and later Catholic friends invited me to go to church with them. My prayer horizons broadened.

My first out-of-comfort-zone prayer experience came when a Pentecostal church invited the youth quartet I was in to sing.

Now those folks knew how to make a quartet stand up and *sang*. I had a great time, but the most amazing thing to me was their prayer time. The band kept right on playing and when the preacher said, "Let's pray." everybody did, out loud and at the same time. Then a man started praying really loud in words that sounded foreign.

After he finished, the preacher prayed the interpretation, which was just as fascinating to me as the speaking in tongues. Needless to say, I had a hard time keeping my eyes closed during that prayer time.

Later, I was invited to attend mass in a Roman Catholic Church. It was the other end of the spectrum from the Pentecostal service. I was impressed with their reverence for Jesus, but thought the service was ritualistic and spiritually dead. Of course, it was dead to me because I had no idea what the rituals meant.

One thing in particular about the Catholic service that offended my evangelical upbringing was the reading of prayers from the little prayer books that resided next to the little hymnals in the pew racks.

These experiences convinced me that, though I was satisfied with the denomination of my parents, there was a lot more to prayer than what I'd been experiencing in my home church.

About that time, I came in contact with the book by Rosalind Rinker, *Prayer, Conversing with God*. As I remember it, our youth leader introduced us to this form of conversational group prayer during our weekly Bible study.

Rinker's book gives several guidelines for conversational small group prayer. Generally, the group members pray multiple short prayers about one topic at a time rather than long monologue prayers. (This form of prayer was discussed under the heading Topical Praying in chapter 12.)

This was prayer that seemed real to me. It gave God the opportunity to really move in our midst and the youth group experienced revival. A number of kids were saved and several of us surrendered to the ministry.

I started college on fire for God and excited to be right in the middle of His plan for my life. Little did I know that the devil had a plan too. During my freshman year, I had a traumatic experience involving moral failure by a minister whom my family had admired and trusted. There's no purpose in elaborating the details, but it left a secret root of bitterness in me that began eating away my spirit like a hidden cancer. The first thing to die was my prayer life. I kept up the appearance of a super-Christian, but inside, my faith was evaporating.

I married my best friend, led a successful youth ministry in a large church, finished my undergraduate degree and was half way through seminary before I hit bottom. One afternoon, sitting in the car on a Dairy Queen parking lot, I admitted to my wife that I no longer believed in God. I was walking the walk and talking the talk, but had gradually become a closet agnostic. I could say a public prayer as fine as anyone even though I hadn't talked to God in years.

I left the ministry and went to work in construction. As I continued to sink into bitterness, I came to the point of literally hating God. One Sunday I agreed to attend worship with my wife and had to literally sit on my hands during the sermon to control my anger. I wanted to jump up and yell at the preacher that everything he was saying was a lie.

Three things protected and sustained me during the spiritual darkness that engulfed me for the next few years:

➢ The consistent Christian walk of my wife and family.
➢ The patient grace of God.
➢ The constant prayers of everyone who loved me.

I had no joy during that period of my life even though I would never have admitted it. I couldn't smile, even when I tried. In the end, it was the longing for the genuineness and truth of my earlier relationship with the Lord that brought me back to my knees.

One afternoon, alone at home, I got on my knees and prayed this simple prayer, "Dear God, I don't know for sure if you exist, but if you do, I'm sorry for the things I've said and done against you. I still have a lot of questions and some day I wish you would answer them, but if you don't, I'll accept that because I'm ready to let you be God in my life again."

That was it. No flashes of lightning or exhilarating emotion. Just a quiet renewal in my spirit as I re-established my conversational relationship with God by confessing my sin and submitting my will to His.

I came out of that experience with a commitment to authentic prayer. However, years later, during preparation for a sermon on the cleansing of the temple, I became convicted by Jesus' words:

…It is written, 'My house is a house of prayer,'…
Luke 19:46 (NKJV)

Our church was active and happy, but no one was walking out of our worship services saying, "Wow, that's a house of prayer."

As I pleaded with the Lord for direction, He convicted me about my attitudes toward those Pentecostal and Catholic services I'd attended as a teenager. He pressed on my heart that He liked the congregational prayer they were doing a whole lot more than the nothing we were doing.

We had prayers during our worship services as much as other churches, but He was convicting me about leading my whole congregation to pray, not just the folks that prayed publicly and came to prayer meetings. I remembered the wonderful conversational prayer I'd experienced as a teen, but couldn't see how to apply it to a congregation.

I tried everything I could think of. I built prayer benches at the front of the auditorium, preached a series of sermons on prayer, and expanded our prayer ministry, but nothing changed. The pew sitters were still sitting right where they always had, doing just what they had always done: watching and listening.

About that time, the church graciously gave me a two-month sabbatical. I traveled the country attending great churches. One of my goals was to see how these famous congregations prayed. I was disappointed. They had wonderful worship and great preaching, but no congregational prayer. Don't misunderstand; these were great praying churches with hundreds of people involved in their prayer ministries. However, the people in the pew were not being led to pray any more than the folks in my church.

God was breaking my heart for His people. I'd been their pastor for ten years, long enough to know that the majority of them didn't have an adequate prayer life. I had to find a way to help them all encounter God through prayer.

The light began to come on when the Heavenly Father finally got a simple truth through to me.

God's people want to pray.

At first, I was really confused by this revelation because I'd been struggling to get folks to pray. It was like pulling teeth. They wanted to do everything but pray. What was God saying?

Here's what the Lord explained to me. Followers of Christ want to talk to their Heavenly Father, but most of them are afraid to speak in public and they all hate being bored. Now I saw the problem. Most public prayer boils down to those two things, one person making a spiritual speech, while everyone else is bored.

When I started looking out across my congregation with the assurance that almost everyone there had come into the room with a desire to talk with the Lord, I began to see our prayer time in a whole different light.

It wasn't a matter of making them pray or praying for them, it was all about letting them pray.

As I began trying to apply this principle, I quickly realized that my Sunday morning pastoral prayer was a hindrance to congregational prayer because the congregation wasn't praying with me. I tried lots of things, but didn't feel like we were making much headway until one Sunday morning when I made a surprising discovery.

I realized that I'd been having an effective congregational prayer time for years without even realizing it. It was what we called the *invitation* at the conclusion of the service.

After my sermon, with music playing softly, I would have the congregation bow, then guide them through a time of reflection. Just before I presented the altar call, I would guide them through a prayer of repentance and surrender to the will of Christ. I led this prayer similar to what I now call prayer by suggestion.

Applying these same techniques to the pastoral prayer eventually produced the techniques detailed in Part 3 of this book. It also began a new chapter in my pulpit ministry and the prayer life of our congregation. It was a dream come true, a passion fulfilled.

I'll never forget the Sunday one of the young fathers stopped as he shook my hand on his way out of the sanctuary. "I don't listen to your pastoral prayer anymore." He had my full attention as he continued, "You get me started talking to the Lord and I just don't hear anything else you say."

I said, "Hallelujah!"

The next step of my pilgrimage came years later, after I'd left the pastorate and begun my writing career. I was two months into a rural interim pastorate when the chairman of the deacons stopped me and said, "The way you do the pastoral prayer, I like it. That's the way it ought to be done."

I love men like that. He had encountered something new, given it prayerful consideration, and made a decision.

I thanked him for his kindness, but his words reverberated in my spirit for days. I knew that the way I led prayer was good for folks and pleasing to God, but this rural deacon had said, "That's the way it *ought* to be done." I didn't realize it until later, but my pilgrimage had become a crusade for the revival of congregational prayer.

STUDY GUIDE:

1. The followers of Christ want to talk to their Heavenly Father, but most of them are afraid to

   _____ _____ _____ and they all hate being _____.

Discussion question: For every hour of worship in your church, how much time do you estimate the average person actually prays during the service? How much time do you think it should be? Why?

Chapter 22

The Posture of Prayer

Body Language Speaks Your Heart

Does God actually pay more attention if you kneel or raise your hands?

There are several physical positions associated with prayer. Is one better than the other? Does God actually pay more attention if you kneel or raise your hands? How do you decide what's appropriate for a given situation?

Consider these prayer position possibilities:

1. Sitting
2. Standing
3. Kneeling
4. Laying prostrate on the floor
5. Hands raised toward heaven
6. Hands held level with palms up
7. Hands clasped
8. Hands held flat together
9. Head bowed
10. Head raised
11. Eyes closed
12. Eyes open

Some of these are straight out of the Bible and some are traditions that have developed over the centuries. If my calculations are right, there are sixty-four possible combinations to choose from, so what do you do? In your private devotions, the answer's simple - you do what your heart feels. When leading others, however, a

Biblical understanding is helpful. Here are a few scriptures that give some insight.

Come, let us **bow** down in worship, let us **kneel** before the Lord our Maker; for he is our God and we are the people of his pasture, the flock under his care.
Psalms 95:6-7 (NIV)

Then David said to the whole assembly, "Praise the Lord your God." So they all praised the Lord, the God of their fathers; they **bowed** low and fell **prostrate** before the Lord and the king.
1 Chronicles 29:20 (NIV)

Ezra praised the Lord, the great God; and all the people **lifted their hands** and responded, "Amen! Amen!" Then they **bowed** down and worshiped the Lord with their faces to the ground.
Nehemiah 8:6 (NIV)

From these and many other scriptures, we get a picture of how people in Biblical times interpreted different body positions.

Sitting:

Sitting, for instance, was not associated with prayer or worship. There's no mention of chairs in or around the temples of the Old or New Testaments. For that matter, other than the thrones, no chairs are mentioned in the heavenly throne room.

Chairs were scarce in Biblical times. Without machinery to mass produce them, they were expensive and unavailable to the masses. Even homemade stools were scarce. Most sitting was done on the floor, so sitting on a chair was associated with a person of authority, such as a judge sitting on a throne. To sit in his presence was disrespectful unless invited to do so. The only time sitting was a sign of submission was when sitting on the floor at someone's feet. Nowhere is it associated with prayer.

Most of us do a great deal of our praying while sitting. Is this scripturally acceptable? Yes. If people in the Bible had been blessed with chairs, they would have sat just as much as we do.

Standing:

Many worship leaders and worshipers today make a big deal about standing during worship. There's nothing spiritual about standing during worship or prayer. It can be concluded that because of the absence of chairs, our ancient ancestors did stand much of the time, but like sitting, standing's not directly associated with prayer or worship in the Bible. They stood because they had nothing to sit on.

There's another issue concerning standing that worship leaders need to keep in mind. Short people can't see over tall people when everyone's standing. My wife is 5'0" and it doesn't matter where she sits, five tall people who stand during every chorus always sit right in front of her. It must be a law of nature. She might as well have a box over her head.

I mentioned to my wife one day that I didn't think there were chairs in the heavenly throne room and that we would probably stand during the worship services there. Her reply, "Well God better resurrect us all the same height because when I go to church in Heaven, I want to see."

Unlike sitting and standing; **bowing, kneeling, and prostrating** one's self is mentioned often in scripture and related directly to prayer and/or worship. Most often these postures were spontaneous and personal expressions of humility and submission to God. There are numerous examples of large groups using these positions too. With large groups, however, it usually involved a crisis or special ceremony.

Head bowed or raised?

Bowing of the head in prayer helps us focus our attention away from our surroundings and is a position of submission. No wonder it's mentioned so often in scripture.

For many Christians, it's the most common bodily position associated with prayer, to the extent that they would have a hard time praying any other way. In their tradition, virtually every public prayer is preceded by instructions to bow for prayer.

However, for others, praying with face lifted is more common. In fact, many congregations use the face lifted posture almost exclusively.

Which should you use? The one that's appropriate for your situation and expresses the heart of the people you're leading.

Both traditions would do well to be open to the other. As mentioned, the bowed head is a position of submission and is appropriate for prayers of confession and supplication. The face lifted is a position of open communication and fellowship. It's more appropriate for prayers in which the worshiper is receiving God's blessing.

There is an issue of pride here that should prompt anyone who raises their face to God to examine their heart first. More discussion of this issue follows in the section on praying with eyes open or closed.

Kneeling

Kneeling is always appropriate in private devotions and every sanctuary should make provision for individuals to kneel. If you're leading a group and want to give them opportunity to kneel during the prayer time, consider these issues.

➤ In most groups, there are some who can't kneel at all because of physical problems.
➤ The average person can only kneel for a short time unless provided with a very good kneeling rail.
➤ Kneeling can produce modesty issues.

Because of these and other matters, it would be unusual for a whole group to get on their knees. The best thing is to make preparations so they can kneel, then give them the option to kneel if they want.

There's a piece of hardware that evangelical Christianity needs to go back and borrow from its Catholic ancestors - the pew mounted kneeling rail. If pew salesmen would market these to all churches, they might find a big market.

Prayer rails and benches in the altar area are good, but having rails on the back of every pew is superior. The emphasis in evangelical Christianity is on getting people to the altar. That comes from the camp meeting heritage, which shouldn't be abandoned. However, if there's to be a revival of congregational prayer, it will take place in the pew.

Prostration:

In our culture, prostration is appropriate for private devotions, but not group prayer. Many of us have found ourselves flat on the floor crying out to the Lord in times of extreme personal hardship or spiritual warfare. And I have been in a few small group prayer meetings where some participants spontaneously prostrated themselves. However, it's not a posture of prayer I would ever encourage in group prayer. I don't know of any place in scripture where someone's instructed to prostrate themselves. It's always spontaneous.

Raised hands:

Raising hands toward heaven has several meanings that haven't changed much in thousands of years. It was used in association with vows just as it is in courts today. It was a sign of blessing much as you see the Pope raise his hand to bless crowds of worshipers. And it was a sign of praise during worship, perhaps exactly as it's used today.

Raised hands during prayer is a little different than during a praise song, however. Hands raised in praise represent something given to God. In prayer, they represent a reaching out for assistance, much as a toddler reaches out and up toward a parent when hurt or wanting attention. This reaching motion is so natural and ingrained from childhood, it's no wonder that it's so widely used.

Generally, you won't instruct people to raise or not raise their hands during prayer. It will be left up to the individual.

Sometimes raised hands become an issue within a group. If you suspect tension, prepare a Bible study that includes a handout of pertinent scriptures. To get the attention of those who think everyone should raise their hands, you might start with the first half of the following verse:

When you spread out your hands, I
will hide My eyes from you; Even though
you make many prayers, I will not hear.
Your hands are full of blood.
Isaiah 1:15 NKJV

This passage is not so much about raised
hands as it is about having your heart right when
you pray. And that's what you want to
communicate to your group.

For those who tend to look down their nose
at the unrestrained hand raisers, you might
include a review of 2 Samuel 6 in which Michal
is critical of King David for his undignified
worship.

It also might be helpful to have a discussion
about body language and fetishes. (see last
sections of this chapter) The point is to help them
see that God sees past the position of their body
to the attitude of their heart.

Clasped hands:

Most of us talk with our hands. As we
speak, our hands are forming visual illustrations
of the concepts we are trying to communicate. So
why do we eliminate this natural part of
expression by clasping our hands during prayer?
The obvious answer is that we have our eyes
closed, but there may be some ancient traditions
involved too.

Certainly one of the most copied pictures of
all time is *The Praying Hands* by Albrecht Durer
of the fifteenth century AD. Legend has it that
the hands are those of his brother who worked in
the mines to pay for Albrecht's education.
Whatever the truth about the picture, it is known
that Durer was one of the first artists to make
extensive use of printed pictures and, thereby,
became one of the few artists who could support
himself financially. This explains how this one
picture has so influenced personal prayer since
the early days of the reformation.

However, the practice of folding the hands
together in prayer can be dated a thousand years

before the reformation to the fifth century AD
and the Saxons.

Going back much farther than that, we find
in Jewish tradition that the priests joined their
hands in a peculiar way as they quoted prayers
and blessings with the congregation. This goes
back at least as far as ancient synagogues and
probably the Old Testament temple. No doubt,
this practice was slightly different from place to
place and time to time, but it involved the
touching together of the index fingers while
interlocking the others. This symbol of praying
hands became so associated with the priesthood,
that it's etched on many of their ancient
tombstones.

Clasping your hands is a very natural
position of prayer and a centuries old tradition,
but isn't mandated in scripture. Though a part of
some liturgies, it should not be construed as
something deemed necessary by God.

Open or closed eyes:

Closing of the eyes is not directly mentioned
in scripture in relation to prayer, but can be
inferred by the frequent references to bowing. On
the other hand, looking someone in the face was
a sign of equality and therefore not appropriate
for communion with God. Consider this verse.

Who is it you have insulted and
blasphemed? Against whom have you
raised your voice and **lifted your eyes
in pride**? Against the Holy One of Israel!
2 Kings 19:22 (NIV)

Praying with your head raised and your eyes
open isn't a sin, but care should be taken. The
prophets of the Old Testament (Zephaniah 3:11)
and Jesus in the New Testament (Luke 18:11),
made it clear that the Lord has a strong distaste
for pride and arrogance. Examine your motives.

Having said that, it can be beneficial to open
your eyes in some prayer situations. For instance,
if you're leading a vespers in a location of great
natural beauty, suggesting that the group pray

with their eyes open would be appropriate. In general, any time there's something to look at that draws attention to or glorifies God, praying with your eyes open is an option.

Body language:

Body language, as a form of communication, is often more revealing of our inner being than what we say. If you think of yourself at home watching a favorite movie, at your child's sporting event, and at the funeral of a loved one; you'll see three very distinct body languages that communicate what's going on in your mind.

The verse above (2 Kings 19:22) applies directly to a pagan king who had blasphemed God, but reveals that God does notice body language. However, it's the attitude of one's heart, which the body language reveals, that really concerns the Lord.

Also He (Jesus) spoke this parable to some who trusted in themselves that they were righteous, and despised others: "Two men went up to the temple to pray, one a Pharisee and the other a tax collector. The Pharisee **stood** and prayed thus with himself, 'God, I thank You that I am not like other men-- extortioners, unjust, adulterers, or even as this tax collector. I fast twice a week; I give tithes of all that I possess.' And the tax collector, **standing** afar off, **would not so much as raise his eyes** to heaven, but **beat his breast**, saying, 'God, be merciful to me a sinner!' I tell you, this man went down to his house justified rather than the other; for everyone who exalts himself will be humbled, and he who humbles himself will be exalted."
Luke 18:9-14 (NKJV)

Both of the men in this parable are standing as they pray, but the body language of the tax collector reveals a great difference in the condition of his heart. His heart was broken in remorse for his sin, while the Pharisee was so blinded by his pride that he could not see the sin of his own arrogance.

Do not manipulate worshipers into using a prayer posture of your choice. Instead, create an atmosphere of spiritual freedom and provide them with opportunities to pray in a way that expresses what they feel in their heart.

Fetishes:

Human beings are fetish prone. We're always looking for shortcuts, and that's just as true in worship as anywhere else. Any of the postures of prayer can become a fetish. For instance, if a person had a particularly moving experience during a service in which they stood much of the time, standing can easily become a fetish for them. Standing during subsequent services tends to bring back those feelings and therefore helps them enter into an attitude of worship more easily.

We're all like this. Worship fetishes can be anything from speaking in tongues to singing with your eyes closed. A particular action becomes a shortcut that produces immediate spiritual memories or feelings. The problem is that it eventually becomes little more than a habit.

I once saw a lady demonstrate this perfectly. It was during the morning worship of a conference I was attending. We were into the fourth or fifth chorus, everyone was standing, the congregation was singing beautifully, and many worshipers had their hands raised. I noticed some extra motion by a lady sitting near me and couldn't help but glance her way. Her left hand was waving back and forth above her head, but not as a result of great spiritual motivation. It seemed that her cell phone was ringing in her purse, but she was doing her best to keep that left hand held high while rummaging around in the purse with her right hand.

There's nothing wrong with having a particular prayer or worship posture that blesses you as long as you don't get in a rut with it, understand that it has no inherent power, and don't spiritualize it to the point that you think anyone who doesn't share your fetish is out of touch with God.

STUDY GUIDE:

1. The positions of bowing, kneeling, and prostrating one's self are all mentioned in scripture in situations related to prayer. True or False

2. The Bible indicates that God does notice our _____ _____ when we pray, but really cares more about our _____ which it reveals.

Discussion question: Why do you think raising hands during prayer and worship bothers some people?

Chapter 23

Cell Phones in the Throne Room

Stop Interrupting God

Pastors and worship leaders, who would never intentionally be disrespectful to God, do so weekly by interrupting Him to do things of lesser importance.

Few inventions have influenced society as significantly as the cellular telephone. They make commerce more efficient and reaching out to one another easier than ever. But with all the benefits, comes a pervasive gadget that is often a nuisance and sometimes dangerous.

Theaters, restaurants, and even church bulletins carry reminders to silence them. Many hospitals insist that they be turned off, and cell phones have been involved in so many fatal accidents that some states outlaw them while driving.

Knowing all this, we still find it hard to turn them off. Even though they have answering machines built right in, we just hate the thought of not answering a call. And when we do answer, no matter where we are, we seem to think the rest of the world can be put on hold. We've all had the experience in a restaurant where someone talks so loudly on their cell that everyone within twenty feet is forced to listen in.

If you were invited to the oval office of the president, would you turn off your cell phone? Can you imagine yourself interrupting the leader of the western world to say, "Excuse me Mr. President, I have a call…Hello…Yeah…Sure, I'll pick some up on the way home. Guess where I am…."

Hopefully we all see how totally inappropriate that would be, but if you wouldn't treat the president that way, why do you treat the creator of the universe that way? "Oh no", you say? You think you would never be so rude? Consider the average evangelical blended worship service.

The segments of the service in **bold** are those that, if done well, will draw people into the presence of God and can be considered worship. (For our purposes, the sermon doesn't count.)

Prelude		
Opening set of songs	6	minutes
Announcements	4	minutes
Second set of songs	5	minutes
Pastoral prayer	1.5	minutes
Welcome of guests	1.5	minutes
Promotion of special event	3	minutes
Third set of songs	5	minutes
Offertory prayer	0.5	minutes
Offertory music	2.5	minutes
Special Music	3	minutes
Sermon	25	minutes
Prayer	1	minute
Altar Call	2	minutes
Closing remarks	5	minutes
Benediction	1	minute

	Total:	66.	minutes
Total Prayer:	4	minutes
Altar Call:	2	minutes
Total Music:	22.5	minutes
Sermon:	25	minutes
Announcements & Promotions:	7	minutes

Do you see the problem? Imagine God sitting on the throne as the congregation comes into the throne room worshiping Him. Now try to see what happens in that typical worship service from His perspective.

➤ The congregation enters singing wonderful songs of praise that bring Him pleasure.
➤ Then the worship leader turns to the Lord and says, "Excuse us Father, we need to step out for a few minutes to make some announcements. You know the annual banquet is coming up, and of course we have to remind everyone of visitation. We'll be right back."

➤ After a few minutes, the congregation sings their way back into the throne room. Then the pastor steps up and prays the pastoral prayer about world problems and folks in the hospital. The congregation mills about and most drift out of God's presence, bored and thinking about lunch.
➤ When the pastor says "Amen", he turns his back on God and ushers the remaining congregation out of the throne room again. He welcomes visitors and gives them instructions on how to register their presence.
➤ Then standing between the congregation and the entrance to the throne room, he asks for their undivided attention as he promotes the denominational mission offering.
➤ When the pastor steps aside, the worship leader guides the congregation back into the throne room a third time. The music and praise are beautiful to the Lord's ears, but soon the worship is stopped again. And on it goes.

Have I made my point? There's nothing wrong with announcements, welcoming visitors, or taking an offering. The problem arises when those things interrupt worship. Pastors and worship leaders, who would never intentionally be disrespectful to God, do so weekly by interrupting Him to do things of lesser importance. It's as if God's children don't respect Him enough to turn off their cell phones in the throne room.

Why do Christians act like this? Why have so many become satisfied with services that never let them spend quality time with their Heavenly Father? Satan surely has something to do with it. The evil one, little by little, has deceived them into thinking what they're experiencing week to week is all there is. How sad.

What should you do about it? Depends on who you are. If you're in a position to actually influence the order of service in your church, start by analyzing your worship service. Appendix 2, Conducting a Worship Service

Profile, is a good starting place. Rearrange the service so that once the congregation is led into the Lord's presence, they stay there for at least twenty minutes without interruption. See Appendix 1, Planning a God-Centered Worship Service.

If you're not involved in the planning of worship, but think this book would be helpful to those who are, buy them a copy, take them out to lunch, and share with them what you've learned.

Ministers are given lots of books and usually don't have time to sit down and read the whole thing. You'll need to sell them on it with a personal testimony and a note telling them how it blessed you and which parts of the book you think will be of most interest to them.

After a couple of weeks, ask them what they thought about it. Don't be surprised if they haven't had time to look at it yet. Ask again later. Be patient, but don't be afraid to keep asking. It's important.

STUDY GUIDE:

1. There's nothing wrong with announcements, welcoming visitors, or taking an offering. The

    problem arises when those things _____ worship.

Discussion question: During the most recent worship service in your church, what do you estimate was the longest segment of uninterrupted worship? Why do you think the author recommends at least twenty minutes of uninterrupted worship.

PRAYER GUIDE by Lowell Snow

Chapter 24

The Forgotten Altar of Prayer

Empowered by Holy Fire

Bringing people into a right relationship with God was the purpose of the sacrificial system, but bringing them into a personal relationship with Him through prayer is His ultimate goal.

And the whole multitude of the people was praying outside at the hour of incense. Luke 1:10 (NKJV)

A young priest stands on a raised porch with his back to huge golden doors. On either side, bronze pillars stand three stories in height. From a distance he appears to be in a blazing fire, engulfed in dazzling golden light as the mid-morning sun reflects off the gold and polished bronze.

But for the slow swinging of his bronze censer, he is motionless. A curl of smoke wafts from the censer and is carried away by the cool morning breeze as his eyes follow a clean white lamb that's being carried across the small courtyard. The lamb looks up and bleats fearfully. *"Does it know?"*

Motion catches his attention and he looks over the wall of this courtyard to the one beyond. Two priests are opening the gates. As worshipers pour in, he looks beyond that gate to the outer courtyard. The white pillars of the porches are a vivid contrast to surrounding Judean sandstone hills. In the porch shadows, venders are already selling their wares. Even though they're a hundred cubits away, he can hear the den of their commerce, punctuated with laughter and shouting. *"Do they know?"*

Scattered among them are pilgrims. Some are men with children on their shoulders. They're looking in this direction, trying to see over the walls that separate them from this temple of

Jehovah God. *"Gentiles,"* thinks the priest by the golden doors, *"Do they know?"*

Within the central courtyard, the crowd of Jewish worshipers is growing. Most, like the Gentile pilgrims in the outer courtyard, hang back, hoping to get a better view over the wall that separates even them from their own temple. Many of the men have their sons beside them, perhaps their first experience so close to the earthly dwelling of the Almighty. Some have tethered lambs, while many carry little cages with sacrificial birds bought from the venders. *"Do they know?"*

Everything's ready within the inner courtyard of the priests. Ripples of heat rise from the blazing fire within the altar of sacrifice. The lamb is bleating continually as a priest holds a knife to its throat. Everyone, even the vendors in the outer courtyard, grows quiet now. The only sound is the bleating of the lamb.

Then silence. No laughter, no talking, no bleating, as the life blood of the lamb flows away.

The priests by the altar begin to prepare the limp body with swift efficiency. Shortly, one of them carries the carcass of the lamb up the steps of the altar, holds it high and announces that the morning sacrifice has been made on behalf of the priests. Then he places it on the grate directly over the fire. It crackles and sizzles as a column of pungent smoke rises.

The vendors turn back to their work, and pilgrims begin talking again as they point toward the golden doors. The priest with the censer watches the smoke ascend toward the heavens, then takes another look at the worshipers. Most of them are still watching the doors, hoping for a glimpse inside. He turns as assistants strain against the massive weight and the doors creek open allowing sunshine to flood in. Reflecting off the gold covered floor, every corner of this sacred room is filled with shafts of brilliant light. Ooos and ahs can be heard from the courtyards.

The doors open, the assistants stand motionless, waiting to close them as soon as the priest enters with the morning incense. Standing now before perhaps the most beautiful display of wealth on earth, he looks down at the censer and gives it a little shake. A whiff of smoke emerges, accompanied by a few sparks. All seems ready. He glances at the assistants, but they are spellbound by the golden glory within the doorway. *Do they know?*

He steps in and is welcomed by the smell of bread and incense. As he walks slowly into this sanctuary of holy solitude, the doors close behind him and the golden opulence is suddenly transformed into silent reverence. Halfway across the room, he stops, gaze fixed on the object of his assignment, the altar of incense.

All of his life he's waited for this moment. Ever since his father explained the sacrificial system to him as a boy, he's yearned for the opportunity to enter the Holy Place and offer the incense of prayer. His father had said, "You will offer a thousand animals at the altar of sacrifice, but until you stand before the altar of incense, the golden altar of prayer, and realize you're only steps from the Shekinah, only then will you know. Only then will you understand."

"Know what, father?" he had asked those many years ago.

"I can't tell you my son, for there are no words to describe the heart of God."

His trembling legs lose their strength and he falls to his knees, ten steps short of his task. He stares at the floor, no longer able to raise his eyes to the altar. He feels alone, sinful, afraid. In his mind the ancient names of Nadab and Abihu wrap themselves around his deepest fears. Those early priests were both killed by God because they came before this altar inappropriately.

He thinks of the pilgrims in the courtyards, now reaching out to touch the walls that separate them from this sacred place. He's watched them countless times. Some will kneel, others will stand, but they all will try to touch the wall. Some are sick. Others are broken hearted or afraid. A few are just thankful. All are seeking an encounter with God.

Do they know? Do they know the heart of God? Do they know what I don't? How am I different from them? Oh God, I am not righteous.

The gentiles praying in the outer court may be more worthy than I. He wishes for his father.

As he stoops lower and lower he begins to weep, then feels the heat of the censer next to his face. Turning to the hot globe, he finds the glowing coals greeting his gaze through the perforations of the censer.

"Holy fire." The words of his father come to him. "None of us is worthy to approach the holiness of the Lord. When it comes your time to stand before the veil, you will carry holy fire from the altar of sacrifice. By His grace, it will protect you from the Shekinah."

Slowly he stands and walks the final steps to the far end of the temple. Before him, a small golden altar. Behind that, the veil, stretching upward toward the gilded ceiling. Behind that…God.

Hands shaking slightly, he pours the coals from the censer into the shallow bowl, which is the top of the altar. Every motion is the exact replica of those rehearsed over and over with his father, but his thoughts are random, out of control. Every sense is heightened. However, one thought, one emotion, one sense saturates every other; God is only steps away, waiting, watching.

The fire ready, he hangs the golden tongs back in their place.

"Ahhh."

He jerks back toward the altar. Had he heard something? He's confused. It was something, but maybe not a sound that he heard with his ears. He stares at the veil. There's no sound from within the temple, only the distant murmuring of the pilgrims praying in the courtyards.

Glancing back and forth between the veil and altar, he retrieves a bag of incense from his belt, opens it and prepares to pour it on the fire. As he holds it over the coals, suddenly his thoughts fall into place: the glory of the temple, the blood of the sacrificial lamb, the holy fire, the pilgrims praying in the courtyards, the altar of prayer here only steps from the veil, and now the incense.

His father had been right. Only now does he understand. Only now does he know the heart of God. *The Father wants to talk with His children.*

He truly loves this. Not the blood and death, not the gold and splendor, the prayer. It's all about the prayers.

"Ahhh."

Paralyzed by the revelation, he feels like Adam in the Garden of Eden, waiting for God to come strolling by for a casual conversation. How had he missed this? All his life he had said ritualistic prayers. Never had he thought that God wanted to communicate with him personally.

Now he gazes at the veil, mouth open, trying to turn his thoughts into words. "Lord, I see now that you are a gracious Father who loves to talk with His children. Many of them have gathered today and are calling out to you, which I now realize brings you great pleasure. This incense represents their prayers."

As he shakes the incense onto the glowing coals, the sweet smoke rises before the veil and drifts out the windows next to the ceiling, ascending toward the heavens.

"Ahhh."

For most Christians, the altar of incense is overshadowed by the altar of animal sacrifice. This is understandable, but unfortunate, because the altar of incense is the only part of the temple that's so important to God that it's replicated in the throne room of Heaven directly in front of the throne.

> **Another angel, who had a golden censer, came and stood at the altar. He was given much incense to offer, with the prayers of all the saints, on the golden altar before the throne. The smoke of the incense, together with the prayers of the saints, went up before God from the angel's hand. Revelation 8:3-4 (NIV)**

The altar of incense was, and still is, the altar of prayer.

Looking at it from God's point of view, from inside the holy of holies, this golden altar of prayer was actually more central to temple worship than the altar of sacrifice. Located inside the temple directly in front of the veil that separated the holy of holies from the rest of the temple, nothing - other than the Ark of the Covenant - had a more prominent location.

Every morning and evening, just after a perfect one year old lamb was sacrificed on the large altar outside, a priest would come inside the temple and burn incense on this eighteen-inch square, three-foot tall altar. David had this daily ritual in mind when he wrote:

O Lord, I call to you; come quickly to me. Hear my voice when I call to you. May my prayer be set before you like incense; may the lifting up of my hands be like the evening sacrifice. Psalms 141:1-2 (NIV)

The people never had an opportunity to approach this important altar because only the priest could go into the temple, but they knew it was there and what it meant. The smoke from the incense was a symbol of their prayers. As they remained outside, saying their prayers, the smoke from the altar of incense went up before God inside.

The two altars, the altar of sacrifice outside the temple and the altar of incense inside, were directly related. Incense could not be placed on the altar inside until the lamb was sacrificed outside and the only fire that could be used for the altar of incense had to come from the altar of sacrifice.

Do you remember that God killed the two sons of Aaron because they offered 'strange fire' on the altar of incense? (Leveticus10:1) What was the strange fire? Evidently, among other mistakes, they used coals from somebody's campfire rather than the altar of sacrifice.

Do you see their fatal misunderstanding? They thought the authority to go before God resided in themselves as newly ordained priests.

They had failed to see the connection between the bloody sacrifices outside the temple and the holiness of the altar of incense (prayer) inside the temple. Everything on the altar of incense had to be holy. God could tolerate no exceptions.

So what have we learned about this forgotten altar?

➤ The altar of incense was located directly in front of the presence of God.
➤ It was at the heart of daily temple worship.
➤ It was empowered with holy fire from the altar of sacrifice.

It's pretty clear that in the mind and heart of God, prayer was the primary purpose of temple worship.

Most of us have been taught that the purpose of temple worship (which is a picture of God's salvation plan) was to bring people into a right relationship with Him. That's not wrong; it just stops short of God's complete purpose.

Bringing people into *right* relationship was accomplished by the sacrificial system and ultimately the death of Jesus on the cross, but bringing His children into *personal* relationship through prayer is His ultimate goal.

In both testaments the temple is referred to by God as a house of prayer. (Isaiah 56:7, Matthew 21:13) In 2 Chronicles 7:12, He also calls it a house of sacrifice, but His own application of that statement in verse 15 is that He will be attentive to the prayers prayed there.

Do you remember what God did immediately after Christ died? While the body of Jesus was still hanging on the cross, God grabbed the veil that separated the holy of holies and altar of incense, and ripped it in two, top to bottom. Don't you know He had wanted to do that for a long time?

There was no more need for the veil. The veil had represented the power of sin to separate men from God. Now, every person, by faith in Christ, can become a priest, cleansed once and for all by Jesus' sacrifice, and encounter the Heavenly Father personally.

Your ultimate goal as a New Testament prayer guide is not to go into the temple for the people you lead in prayer, but to guide them into the holy of holies to talk with their Heavenly Father themselves.

STUDY GUIDE:

1. The altar of incense is the only part of the temple that's replicated in _____.

2. It's pretty clear (from the layout of the temple) that in the mind and heart of God, _____ was the primary purpose of temple worship.

3. In both testaments the temple is referred to by God as a house of _____.

Discussion question: In your opinion, what's the significance of the veil being ripped open after the death of Jesus?

PRAYER GUIDE by Lowell Snow

Chapter 25

Prayer, the Heart of Worship

Revival of Congregational Prayer

Praise and thanksgiving bring God's people into His presence, but it's by prayer that they take the final step of worship and enter into a personal encounter with Him.

The land is ripe for spiritual harvest, yet the church seems powerless to reap it because the people in the pews are not experiencing an authentic encounter with God.

Many see the seeds of revival blowing in the fresh desire among God's people to pray. All across the land sermons are preached, books published, and new ministries started: calling the faithful to prayer. However, between these seedlings of renewal and the full flowering of revival, prayer must make the leap from prayer closet to sanctuary. The church stands in need of a revival of congregational prayer.

The major roadblock isn't the lack of desire or effort, but the absence of effective prayer guides. In many, if not most churches, there isn't a single person trained in the skills of guiding effective corporate prayer.

Talk to a dozen ministers in your denomination and ask if they were trained in these skills. You'll be surprised, maybe appalled. There are tens of thousands of worship leaders who've spent hundreds of hours learning the ins and outs of music and praise, but not one week in the study of prayer leadership.

Pastors have been taught everything from child psychology to the dangers of higher criticism, but not required to read a single book on effective corporate prayer. No wonder their congregations are languishing in a prayer wasteland.

Pastors and worship leaders who apply the prayer guide skills will make a difference in a world crying out for a personal encounter with the Almighty.

In the previous chapter, The Forgotten Altar of Prayer, we saw that the altar of incense was:

1. Closest to the presence of God
2. Central to Biblical worship
3. Empowered by holy fire from the altar of sacrifice

From this study, we realized that bringing people into a personal relationship with God through prayer was actually the ultimate purpose of the temple system. That's the ultimate purpose of worship today as well.

When Jesus died on the cross, the Father immediately ripped open the veil that separated the holy of holies from the altar of prayer. Thus, He made clear that the purpose of Christ's sacrifice was renewing the personal and conversational relationship that was lost in the Garden of Eden.

This was too much for the temple priests, so they quickly replaced the torn veil. How sad, but what's really sad is that many congregations today act as if the veil is still in place. Like the Old Testament Jews, they come into the courtyard with praise, but never go on into the temple for a personal encounter with the Almighty.

There's much emphasis today on worship. Everyone wants an experience that brings them into the presence of God. That doesn't scare the devil. He knows most of those worshipers are going to be distracted away from the Lord as soon as the music stops.

A wonderful worship service doesn't change people. It draws them toward the Father, but only in prayer can they take the final step that brings them into a life changing encounter with God.

You instinctively know this to be true. If someone comes to you and says they want to become a Christian, you won't sing with them. You may counsel them and instruct them from the Word, but you'll not leave them until you've led them in prayer. Why? Because you know that it's in prayer that they'll encounter God. It's as natural as water running downhill.

On one occasion, I received a call from a stressed-out pastor asking if I could preach for him the following Sunday. The church was going through a difficult time, and he felt that God had given me a message for the church. I'd been praying regularly for this church and did in fact know instantly what God wanted me to do.

I preached the message the Lord had given me, but just as importantly, I used the last ten minutes of that service to lead the congregation in corporate prayer. Using the techniques described in Part 3 of this book, I guided them into the throne room to receive encouragement and blessing from their Savior.

Between services, a graduate student from Eastern Europe caught me in the hall and said, "That was a life changing experience for me." He said that he'd never experienced God in such a dynamic way.

Many others made a point to tell me that the prayer time was exactly what they needed. Several months later, a long time member of the church told me that he kept the CD of that service in his truck so he could listen to it whenever he became discouraged.

People are changed by God when they experience authentic corporate prayer. So why isn't prayer at the heart of every worship service? There may be a thousand answers, but we can be sure that Lucifer's behind most of them. Consider the following reality that seems good at first, but upon closer scrutiny, is revealed as a very successful plot to covertly remove prayer from the sanctuary.

The concept in many evangelical churches is this: bring the people into the presence of God with music, then they'll be ready to hear from God through the preaching or teaching of the Word. I've heard many a pastor or worship leader say this through the years and was taught it on a few occasions in college and seminary. Do you see the problem? This formula doesn't include prayer, does it? So, over many decades, congregational prayer has been reduced to monologue prayer. Instead of each individual having a personal encounter with God, the person leading prayer becomes an Old Testament priest of sorts, having a personal encounter with God as he or she prays a public prayer; and the people sit in the pews listening, much like the worshipers of ancient times had to remain out in the courtyard while the priest entered the temple.

Truly, God has ordained worship and the preaching of the Word. There is no substitute. But it's equally true that God ordained congregational prayer. There is no substitute for corporate prayer either. God's people must be guided from praise into a time of communion with the Lord or worship is incomplete.

Think about services you've experienced where people were truly changed by holy power. At some point in that service, they had an encounter with God. No matter how powerful the preacher, only God can truly change people. In those services, the preacher might not have led a prayer time in the classic sense, but there had to be a time of communion with God if lives were truly changed.

You may have heard it said that the old-time evangelists gave more attention to their invitations than their sermons. That's because their invitations were prayer times, personal encounters with the Almighty. Their sermons may have changed minds, but the prayer times during their invitations were when hearts surrendered to God and lives changed.

However, the heart of the worship service is where congregational prayer really belongs and where it will be most Biblical, most spiritual, and most beneficial.

Some would argue that many of the wonderful choruses we sing today are actually prayers. That's true and many of the great hymns are as well, but this misses the point. A prayer song can't replace a personal encounter with God. Each Christian needs to talk with the Lord individually. For instance, what prayer song or pastoral prayer can express the heart cry of a man whose marriage is falling apart?

Praise and thanksgiving bring God's people into His presence, but it's by prayer that they take the final step of worship and enter into a personal encounter with Him.

If we really want our nation to return to God, the churches across this land must become houses of prayer. The problem seems to be that most congregations have forgotten how to do it. From Bible study leaders and deacons to pastors and television evangelists, public prayer has become little more than spiritual speeches aimed in the direction of God.

The most fearsome war machine of the twentieth century was the nuclear powered attack submarine. The nuclear reactor at the heart of these silent predators is perhaps the most efficient power generation system on earth, but it can't be used for municipal power plants. Why? Because it won't scale-up. In other words it works great in a relatively small application like a submarine or an aircraft carrier, but not a huge

power plant that must produce a thousand times more electricity.

Prayer's a little like that, very powerful on a small scale, (when two or three are gathered in my name…) but complicated and unwieldy on a large scale. That's why corporate prayer comes naturally to a house-church in China, but is difficult in a large congregation. Scaling-up corporate prayer for large groups requires a skilled prayer guide, but it can be done.

Years ago I read the book *Fresh Wind, Fresh Fire*, by Jim Cymbala, pastor of the Brooklyn Tabernacle in New York City. I was impressed by his emphasis on prayer. As the years passed, I kept hearing great things about this church, so I decided to visit and do a profile of the worship service. In the Sunday morning service that I attended with about 4,500 other folks, over 11% of the time was given to prayer. Nearly seven minutes of the two hour and fifteen minute service was congregational prayer. Another thing I noticed was that every segment of congregational music culminated with congregational prayer.

If there's ever to be a revival of congregational prayer, worship leaders, battle weary from decades of the worship wars, are going to have to retrain again, this time in the skills of leading large group prayer.

In fact, it may be that the revival of congregational prayer will be the climactic D-Day of the Worship Wars. When history's written, the absence of corporate prayer will likely be revealed as the real problem that started the war in the first place. It all started when Christians realized they were leaving church spiritually empty and wanted more. Since true congregational prayer had been absent so long, they didn't even know what was missing.

Many of these folks started moving to the contemporary churches that sprang up on the outskirts of towns all across the country. Mainline churches have changed to meet these new expectations, but after all the commotion, the surveys indicate most worshipers are just as spiritually empty when they sit down to lunch on Sunday as their predecessors fifty years ago.

Congregational prayer was lacking in the fifties, and it's nonexistent in many services now. Everywhere, attempts are being made to make worship more relevant, but many of our worship services remain a prayer wasteland. How can we be so blind?

I estimate that 98% of group prayer takes place outside the sanctuary. In some denominations I've documented that it's almost 100%. Christians pray together in Bible classes, meetings, and prayer ministries, but not in their worship centers.

There's a great cry today for God's people to rise up in prayer. Talk to just about any pastor, and he has recently or is currently preaching a series on prayer. There are prayer meetings, prayer ministries, even prayer seminars; but the most logical, Biblical, and spiritually powerful worship time is ignored.

We lament the removal of prayer from the public school, but that tragedy was preceded by the removal of meaningful, congregational prayer from the sanctuary.

> ➤ **There's nothing nearer to the heart of God than His people's prayers.**
> ➤ **There's nothing more worshipful than God's people praying.**
> ➤ **There's no better time to unleash the power of prayer than during worship.**

STUDY GUIDE:

1. Only in _____, can worshipers take the final step that brings them into a life changing _____ with God.

2. God's people must be guided from praise into a time of communion with the Lord or worship is _____.

Discussion question: Contemporary worship tends to have less prayer than traditional services because prayer songs take the place of congregational prayers. Do you feel this is a viable option? Why or why not?

Chapter 26

Guiding a Worship Service Prayer Time

House of Prayer

Keep in mind this picture: pilgrims going through the courtyard with praise, to the temple for forgiveness and conversation with God, then back through the courtyard with celebration and thanksgiving. That order can't be improved on.

As you plan the prayer time for a worship service, keep in mind the temple as a *type* for the order of worship. Pilgrims came to the temple, usually in family groups, singing psalms as they entered the great courtyard that surrounded the Temple. About mid morning, before the pilgrims made their sacrifices, the priests made theirs. This morning sacrifice was also the time of morning prayers, because it was when the holy incense was burned on the altar of incense (altar of prayer), within the temple, directly in front of the holy of holies. As this happened, the pilgrims would face the temple and pray.

After this time of congregational prayer, they would make their own sacrifices. Pilgrims often came prepared to make three kinds: a *sin* offering for the things they had done wrong, a *burnt* offering as a symbol of their dedication to God, and a *peace* offering to celebrate God's goodness.

Today's Thanksgiving Day festivities are a modern-day version of that ancient Hebrew *peace* offering. After the animal was killed and cleaned by the priests, some of the meat was placed on the altar, but most was given back to the family who brought it. This offering also included bread, oil, drink, and salt. The family took the portion returned to them and cooked it within the temple confines, then had a thanksgiving meal together. This is why the courtyard was so huge, and why Jesus was so angry when he found that it had been turned into something more like a flea market.

Keep in mind this picture: pilgrims going through the courtyard singing praise, to the temple for forgiveness and prayer, then back through the courtyard with celebration and thanksgiving. That order can't be improved on.

So, are you ready to bring prayer to its rightful place at the heart of worship? If so, there are three things you need to do right away:

> * Make a commitment to God.
> * Decide who's going to lead.
> * Include prayer in your preparation.

Make a commitment

By now you should have an opinion about congregational prayer. Either you believe every worshiper should be led into a personal encounter with God through prayer or you don't.

If so, are you committed to making a difference? Are you willing to make the effort to become an effective prayer guide? Will you discipline yourself to study and put into practice what you've learned? Can you persevere through confusion and perhaps resistance, to lead your church family into a revival of congregational prayer?

I believe the principles and techniques presented in this book can be of great help to you, but would never ask you to make a commitment to them. Your commitment must be to the Lord and His will for your life. If He has burdened your heart for the revival of congregational prayer and confirmed in your mind that the way of the prayer guide is the way He wants you to proceed, then your commitment should be to Him.

Write down the things God has impressed on your heart that you need to implement. Be as specific as possible.

_____

_____

_____

_____

_____

Now, are you ready to make a commitment? If so, go before Him now, with your list, and make your commitment to be obedient to His direction.

Decide who will lead

Generally, you would expect the pastor to lead the prayer time during worship, but there are exceptions. Many pastors are great communicators, but not good worship leaders. They can pray a powerful monologue prayer, but falter as a prayer guide. Whoever's more gifted in using these prayer guide methods should be the one to lead.

There should never be a turf war between the pastor and worship leader. Any worship service is greatly enhanced when the pastor and worship leader work as a team. The more they communicate and pray together, the more likely the congregation is to have an encounter with God.

If you're a pastor who feels like you're sitting in the eye of the worship war hurricane while the fighting factions swirl around you; being proactive to bring corporate prayer into worship will give you the opportunity to step into the fray with a potentially war-ending strategy.

Include prayer in your planning

How do you begin the planning process for your worship services? Perhaps you start months ahead with a calendar, or maybe a blank outline at 10:00 p.m. Saturday night. However you do it, the prayer time needs to be part of that process from the beginning.

As you plan the worship service, keep in mind this progression of worship that we see in God's design of the temple:

➢ Come into the presence of God with praise and thanksgiving
➢ Encounter Him in prayer
➢ Leave with adoration and celebration

Always schedule at least twenty uninterrupted minutes for this whole process to take place. (Appendix 1) Many services begin with a song or two, followed by welcome and announcements. That's fine, but don't count those songs as part of your twenty minutes of worship.

Preparation:

Before the service:

☐ Write down the needs your congregation is to pray about.

☐ Plan a prayer time consistent with the theme and flow of the worship service. Remember to plan the ending as well as the beginning.

☐ Coordinate with the pastor/worship leader and musicians. The songs should flow into and out of the prayer time without interruption.

☐ Locate a scripture to use for meditation (chapter 13).

☐ Write down and practice a Biblical situation to use for Biblical visualization. (chapter 14)

☐ Write an outline of your prayer time and put it with your sermon notes or music.

When it's time to pray:

➢ Make preparations so that there will be less than two seconds between the prayer time and whatever precedes it.

➢ Invite those who want to kneel to come to the altar if this is possible and appropriate for your congregation. You might begin the scripture meditation as they come to allow time for them to get situated before the prayer begins.

➢ Arrange for music to continue during the prayer time. A gifted instrumentalist playing chord progressions with no melody is best, but unfamiliar songs or even recorded instrumental music can be used. The point is that it should not be a distraction.

➢ Guide them into the presence of God using scripture meditation and/or Biblical visualization.

Salutation:

➢ Begin the prayer with the salutation of your choice. (chapter 5)
➢ Use prayer by suggestion to guide the congregation into personal praise and thanksgiving.

Petition:

➢ Guide them according to your plan and as the Holy Spirit leads you. (See the Sample Prayer in chapter 19 and #2 in Appendix 1 for suggestions.)

➢ Don't neglect the pastoral prayer. Even if he doesn't lead the whole prayer time, he can step in here. This should be a monologue prayer in which he exercises his special position before God to pray for his flock. He might pray about issues outside the church, but it's crucial that the congregation hear their pastor praying for their needs.

➢ Conclude the prayer time according to your plan and in an appropriate time frame. Don't drag it out. You want them to look forward to the next time.

Benediction:

➢ Thank the Lord for His presence.
➢ Conclude with a benediction of your choice. (chapter 5)
➢ Begin worship within two seconds of the benediction. (Remember to keep the prayer time in the center of worship rather than tacked onto the end. Please, please, please: for the sake of reverence to God and for those who are actually talking with Him, don't go directly from "amen" to making an announcement.)

STUDY GUIDE:

1. Old Testament Jews often had meals at church. True or False

2. A worship leader who wants to have more congregational prayer should make a commitment to the four techniques of the prayer guide. True or False.

3. The congregation is more likely to have an encounter with God when the pastor and worship leader _____ and _____ together.

Discussion question: Do you feel that a monologue 'pastoral prayer' should remain a part of the primary weekly worship service? Why?

Conclusion

The temple in Jerusalem was one of the seven wonders of the ancient world yet only a handful of people ever entered it. That temple is gone, but today, by the power of Christ's blood, the wonders of the heavenly throne room are open to all who will come by faith in Jesus. Will you use the principles and skills you've learned in this book to guide others into that awesome place for a personal encounter with Him?

God's people want to pray, but they're tired of stuffy, meaningless public prayer. Most of them have never experienced authentic corporate prayer so they need your help. Try the techniques in this book. Dare to be different. Never again be satisfied with boring, lifeless prayer. Get a vision of the throne room and guide others to it.

STUDY GUIDE:

Discussion question: Write down three things you plan to do differently as a result of studying PRAYER GUIDE.

Appendix I

Quick Guide to Planning a God-centered Worship Service

1. Plan the prayer time as earnestly as you do the praise time. Lead it differently each week.

o   Have a prayer time at the heart of the worship service. Make it the focus of worship rather than a book-end.

o   Have at least 20 minutes of uninterrupted praise and prayer.

o   Try starting the service with upbeat songs and then more meditative songs right before and after the prayer time.

o   The songs should flow into and out of your prayer time seamlessly. The music never stops. Eliminate the dead silence that often precedes and follows prayer.

o   Background music during prayer should not distract the worshipers. Chord progressions with no melody is best.

o   If you're leading prayer, be on the pulpit standing behind the praise leader as he or she finishes the song. Step to the microphone instantly as they move aside. Don't say anything that distracts the people's attention from the Lord. The same's true for the worship leader following the prayer time.

o   Try using other words for prayer like communicate, talk to, etc.

2. Guide the congregation to pray by suggestion rather than example.

o   Try beginning the prayer time by asking the congregation to meditate on the words of a short scripture as you say it several times.

o   Try beginning the prayer time by asking the congregation to visualize a Biblical situation. You might ask them to close their eyes and see themselves in the heavenly throne room, at the foot of the cross, in the garden of the empty tomb, or entering the holy of holies.

o   Forget the idea that you have to be talking to lead people in prayer. Try suggesting something for them to pray about and then be quiet for several seconds while they pray their own prayer.

o   Not every time, but often lead them through the whole sequence of prayer: repentance, praise, thanksgiving, kingdom needs, supplication for others, forgiveness of others, and finally personal needs.

o   Suggest specific things for them to pray about, like: each person seated around them, their Sunday School teacher, church staff, missionaries, government leaders, etc.

o   Don't be afraid to have a time in which you encourage them to listen to God.

o   Try to keep God's people in the habit of talking with the Lord about Kingdom needs and other people more than they do about themselves.

o   Conclude the prayer time with a pastoral prayer in which he focuses on praying for the congregation.

3. Don't forget whose presence you're in.

o   Listen to your own prayers. Is that really what you would say in the throne room of the Heavenly Father?

o   When the congregation needs to pray as one, tell them. Say something like, "There's something we all need to talk to the Lord about now, please pray silently what I pray out loud."

o   Never corrupt prayer by using it to make an announcement or preach a mini-sermon.

PRAYER GUIDE by Lowell Snow

Conducting a Worship Service Profile

See then that you walk circumspectly, not as fools but as wise,

redeeming the time, because the days are evil.

Ephesians 5:15-16 (NKJV)

Success is in the details and a worship service profile documents details of worship that reveal a great deal about how a church does worship and whether it's actually giving quality time to the things it deems most important. For instance, if a congregation says that it wants to be a house of prayer, but spends two minutes in monologue prayer and only fifteen seconds in corporate prayer, but ten minutes on announcements; they've got some significant adjustments to make.

Time is one of the most valuable possessions people have and they are very careful about how they spend it. If there are 100 people in a worship service, that means the congregation, as a whole, is offering one hundred hours to the Lord as a kind of time offering.

One detail that's exposed by a profile is wasted time. One profile revealed thirty-five seconds in which a soloist walked from the congregation to the podium, talked privately with the accompanist, then found a microphone.

Multiply that half minute parade by the 200 people sitting in the pews and it amounted to almost two hours of boredom. This kind of waste can be easily eliminated by training the soloists to always get in position before it's time to sing.

Another issue that many worship leaders don't recognize until they've done a profile is the fragmented service. Even after decades of the Worship Wars, most churches still chop worship into two to five minute segments. The congregation is caught in a revolving door going in and out, in and out, of God's presence.

Then there's bookend prayer, the habit of always putting prayer at the beginning or end of some segment of the service and never in the middle of worship. One of the simple evaluation techniques in the profile evaluation is to put a heart around any prayer preceded and followed by worship.

Whether it's a little issue like dead time between songs or a major one like bringing significant congregational prayer into the heart of worship, a profile gives the church an undeniable picture of what they're doing. A detailed profile followed by an intuitive evaluation can be a powerful tool in helping the church become more Christ-centered and effective.

A simple profile like the one demonstrated in chapter 17, can be very enlightening to any size church. However, if significant change is needed, a more detailed profile followed by in-depth evaluation and reporting is warranted. For this, you'll want to acquire the *Worship Profile Kit* from Stonehouse Creations. It includes:

➤ Worship Service Profile instruction sheets
➤ Profile Evaluation and Report instruction sheets.
➤ Committee meeting agendas for the evaluation process.
➤ Blank work sheets.
➤ Microsoft Excel spreadsheet.
➤ A sample profile and report.

Profile kit available at www.leadingprayer.com

Study Guide Answers

Part 1:
Chapter 1 - conversation, incense or prayer, mercy seat, right, conversational
Chapter 2 - mercy seat or Shekinah glory, group, spiritual speeches, prayer requests
Chapter 3 - False, False, False, guidance or voice, faith
Chapter 4 - saying, leading, guiding, attitude, words, no, see list on the last page of the chapter, method, silently, out loud, background
Chapter 5 - preparation, salutation, petition, benediction, false, invite, talking to, here, throne room, martyred, False, True, will

Part 2:
Chapter 6 – need His help, for, about, announcements and promotions
Chapter 7 – silently, speeches, intentions, False, True
Chapter 8 – top, blessing,
Chapter 9 – God, judge, counselor, priest, True, Listen, analyze, True
Chapter 10 – monologue, circle,True, practice

Part 3:
Introduction to Part 3 – different, more, harder, encounter, God, sin, study, plan, practice, believe
Chapter 11 – False, suggests, silently, do what you've suggested
Chapter 12 – agree, 18, topic, suggestion
Chapter 13 – see the list on the first page of the chapter, distracted, positive side, False
Chapter 14 – faith, parables, picture, True
Chapter 15 – God, each other, sharing, righteousness, well informed

Part 4:
Chapter 16 – needs, see, two or three, topical prayer, False
Chapter 17 – schedule, lesser, notes, confidence, True
Chapter 18 – False, presence of God, needs, get their hearts right, thanks, furniture, trash
Chapter 19 – fifteen, topical prayer, acceptance, comfort,
Chapter 20 – crisis, focus, singular, novice, B

Part 5:
Chapter 21 – speak in public, bored,
Chapter 22 – True, body language, attitude
Chapter 23 – interrupt,
Chapter 24 – Heaven, prayer, prayer
Chapter 25 – prayer, encounter, incomplete
Chapter 26 – True, False, communicate, pray